THE
PSYCHOLOGY
GOD

ERIC J. KOLB, Ph.D.

THE
PSYCHOLOGY
GOD
of

A psychological view of theological concepts

Xulon Press

Xulon Press
2301 Lucien Way #415
Maitland, FL 32751
407.339.4217
www.xulonpress.com

© 2021 by Eric J. Kolb, PhD

All rights reserved solely by the author. The author guarantees all contents are original and do not infringe upon the legal rights of any other person or work. No part of this book may be reproduced in any form without the permission of the author. The views expressed in this book are not necessarily those of the publisher.

Unless otherwise indicated, Scripture quotations taken from the Holy Bible, New International Version (NIV). Copyright © 1973, 1978, 1984, 2011 by Biblica, Inc.™. Used by permission. All rights reserved.

Scripture quotations taken from the King James Version (KJV) – *public domain*.

Printed in the United States of America.

ISBN-13: 978-1-6628-0764-0

Table of Contents

Dedication vii

Chapter One: Introduction 1
    Of Science and Theology 8
    Scientific Method, Data Analysis, and Interpretation 9
    Scientific Psychology 14
    Amaziah: God is my Strength 16
    Focus: A Philosophical Perspective 21
    Nature versus Nurture: Are we only a product of our DNA? . . 26

Chapter Two: The Four Components of the Human:
Heart, Body, Mind, and Soul 32
    The Body 38
    The Heart: The Symbolic Source of Emotion 43
        The Emotional Process 43
        The Theory of Basic Emotions 48
        Fear and Anxiety 55
        Sadness and Depression 61
        Emotional Communication 63
    The Human Mind 71
        Life Stress and Humor 75
    The Human Soul 80

Chapter Three: Models of Development 85
    Freud's Model of Sexual Development 85

Piaget's Model of Cognitive Development.................. 89
Erikson's Model of Social-Emotional Development 92
Kohlberg's Model of Moral Development 98
God's Model of Character Development 108
    The Infant Stage 0-2 years – Abraham to Joseph 111
    The Toddler Stage 2-5 years – Moses to Joshua 112
    The Childhood stage 5-12 years – Joshua to David....... 119
    Adolescence (12-18) – Psalms, Proverbs, Job,
       and the Prophets 124
    Young Adult (18-25) – The Gospels.................... 129
    Adult Stage 25 and older – Act and Epistles............. 134

Chapter Four: Learning Behaviors 140
    Parenting and Discipline................................ 147
    Prayer and Classical conditioning........................ 150

Chapter Five: Faith, Hope, and Love 154
    Faith 154
    Hope 160
    Love 165

Chapter Six: Living and Growing in the Holy Spirit 169
    Chronic Illness... 174

Author's Bio 183
References 185

Dedication

To Him and all who are earnestly seeking and following the Way, the Truth, and the Life.

CHAPTER ONE

Introduction

Both from a scientific and theological perspective, I find the scientific exploration of the universe, life, and the human mind to be an exciting quest and a magnificent calling. Some may claim that one's belief in God contaminates their ability to think scientifically. In fact, studies have shown that individuals with more intuitive thought processes tended to have a belief in spiritualism of some kind, while individuals with more rational thought processes did not (King et al., 2007). I have read these studies, and although I do suspect some bias, the data seem accurate, but the interpretation is quite wrong. Often the data are interpreted in a way that suggests that individuals, who believe in God, tend to do so because they are more intuitive and less rational; and, individuals, who do not believe in God, are more rational and thus smarter (Gervais, 2012; Pennycook et al., 2012; Shenva et al., 2012). However, this is a false and misleading interpretation of the data. A more accurate interpretation of the data is simply that more intuitive individuals have a greater tendency to believe in God than more rational individuals. This is not because intuitive people tend to believe in God, because they do not think rationally, as some may like to interpret. Instead, people, who tend to be more intuitive and less rational in thought, have a greater tendency to believe in God simply because God created man to have relationships.

We are all called initiatively to Him through our intuitive thought process, which develops long before our rational thought process. As such, God created us to believe in Him. However, through the course of our development, we will eventually have to choose between right and wrong. That is when the rational thought process starts to kick in. Humans love to rationalize and honor rational thought. A friend of mine, a great chess player and mathematician, once told me that he would never comprehend how an intelligent person can genuinely believe that a man could come back to life and have the powers of the universe at his disposal. I honestly do understand the question. It does not make sense when one thinks about it simply rationally. Rational thought tells us that this is impossible. However, rational thought is not the only thing that makes us human. God made us Heart, Body, Mind, and Soul and tied them all together with the psychology of God.

Peacocke (1993) suggested that science and theology may be regarded as non-interacting perspectives of reality, which are described in different languages and use entirely different systems and methods of thinking. Furthermore, science and theology have different subject matters. Science attempts to gain an understanding of the nature of the universe, while theology attempts to gain an understanding of the Creator of the universe. Peacocke concluded that because the two disciplines, science and theology, have different subject matters, nature and God, and different study methods, the definitions used in each system may not transpose well between science and theology. Therefore, it is beneficial to study both science and theology and to ponder both the universe and its Creator.

I am a Christian and a scientist. For some, that may be a contradiction. However, I can show that it is not because belief is as much a part of science as it is a part of theology. The scientific method itself incorporates the concept of belief in the process of formulating a hypothesis. Scientists and theologians alike pursue their beliefs, but they do so in a different manner. I believe Jesus Christ died for the sins of the world, that through Him, we can walk with God, which means that we can experience spiritual growth and development. This is what I have been taught in Sunday school, and I have pursued this belief further by studying the Holy Scriptures and science. As a scientist, I believe the scientific method is the best means of acquiring knowledge of all the environments our universe has to offer. However, as I ponder the psychology of God, I do it with the understanding that theology has taught us what to think, while science has taught us how to think.

In the last 150 years, scientific psychology has discovered much about the process of human thinking. However, upon closer investigation of the Holy Scriptures, from the perspective of scientific psychology, I have found that the Bible does indeed teach a great deal about how we as humans should think and how to overcome negative emotions and life stress. Some of these scriptures correspond with the findings of scientific psychology, while others seem to contradict them. The purpose of this book is to contrast and compare scientific psychology with the psychology of God.

My identity, who I think I am, has undergone a development throughout my life, in which each stage has been built upon the previous one. As a child, I was an athlete. In this stage of my life, I learned what it meant to work hard and be physically disciplined. Later, I became a student. I learned to apply my physical discipline to learning at this stage, which one may describe as a cognitive discipline. Later, I became a pilgrim and street performing artist. Through this work, I significantly increased my conscious awareness of my emotional communication, which later became the cornerstone of my therapeutic method. As a psychological counselor, one has to be emotionally disciplined. I have realized that there was not much I needed to do to help those who were empowered by the Holy Spirit. However, I could do little to help those who were not empowered by the Holy Spirit. Finally, as an independent researcher and a man with a broken body, I have come to the understanding that when a person finally chooses to seek help from a psychologist, that is the point in their life in which they are ready to receive the word of God. For when a person is poor in spirit, mourning, timid, empty, beaten, and broken, they do not need Freud, Erickson, James, Skinner, or any other of the great minds of psychology. They need Jesus. That is not to say that the great minds of psychology are not useful; they certainly are. Nevertheless, they are not a replacement for Jesus.

I began this project a couple of years ago, merely in response to an impulse I felt from the spirit of God to write a book about the psychology of God. Through my work as a mental health practitioner, I noticed that while I could only do little for my clients, who did not know the hope that comes from the Grace of God, I only had to do little for those who did. Thus, I asked myself the question, "What is the psychology of God?" This question could be understood in many ways, and I think it is worth discussing it in each conceivable way. Let me begin by explaining what I mean by the "psychology of God." Fundamentally, psychology is the study of behavior, which is very broadly defined as any and all bodily movements. These include the automatically regulated behaviors, such as the beating of the heart, conscious and voluntary behaviors, such as throwing a ball, and emotional communication, which seems to fluctuate somewhere between conscious awareness and non-consciousness. As such, practically everything we do is behavior, whether we are consciously aware of it or not; it is behavior. Skinner and Pavlov would stop there and argue that behavior is all that matters because that is all we can observe in reality. However, scientific psychology has discovered neurotransmitters, core beliefs, cognition, thoughts, emotions, attitude, personality, and many other neurophysiological and metaphysical systems, which are technically not observable behaviors but rather parts of the engine that drives behavior. Thus,' The Psychology of God' refers to God's behavior, as it has been recorded in the Holy Scriptures, as well as how He has created us to behave. Furthermore, I would extend this to include thoughts, emotions, attitude, personality, and the many other systems that drive behavior.

Even if you do not believe in God, science will point out that humans exist and behave in a highly unique manner compared to any other animals. Atheists recognize this vast difference as well but claim it is only a vast difference in the degree of complexity of behavior rather than a difference in the kind of behavior. Christians, such as myself, attribute this difference as evidence of humans being made in God's image. For a while, I thought this book's purpose might be to illustrate the supporting evidence of God's existence through the fields of scientific psychology, as the Reasons to Believe organization does in the field of Biology and Physics. <u>Humans have the same drives, instincts, reflexes, and emotions observed in many other animals. Nevertheless, humans alone have the mental capacity to think about their behaviors in terms of right or wrong and choose to act morally rather than only in response to animalistic impulses.</u> Human behavior is a different kind of behavior, not a difference in the degree of behavioral complexity. While God's existence and evidence from the perspective of scientific psychology are still of great interest to me, it is a subject that deserves its own focus; and one that I hope to address in the near future. For now, I would like to address the topic of the psychology of God from the broadest perspective possible. Even if one does not believe God exists, one can hardly deny that belief in God is unique to humans and has been found to have a significant influence on human behavior, as the many scientific psychological studies cited in this work suggest. Thus, we can focus on contrasting and comparing our scientific understanding of human psychology to the psychology of God that has been illustrated in the Holy Scriptures without getting hung up in unproductive debates. Even if you do not believe that God exists, it is a simple fact that the Bible exists. Upon reading this, some may argue that the Bible is just a book, and one may just as well turn to the works of Shakespeare for guidance. I agree many books offer insight into human emotion and behavior as the Bible does, but that is precisely my point. Just as Edgar (1935) pointed out that Shakespeare's characters demonstrated behaviors that correspond precisely with the clinical symptoms of various psychopathological illnesses 500 years before they were discovered and defined by scientific psychology, the Bible also addresses many aspects of psychology that are discussed in modern scientific psychology. So regardless of whether you hold the Bible as the inspired word of God or merely ancient teaching, one must conclude that only through studying it can one learn from it.

Upon closer examination, I realized that the psychology of God in some aspects might not be significantly different from the scientific psychology that I studied and practiced, while in other aspects, it is. The Bible often speaks of the heart, body, mind, and soul of the human being. However, it does not do so in the form of an easy to follow, step-by-step, psycho-therapeutic method, or development model. To find the psychology of God, one has to look for it and want to find it. Ironically, in this respect, the psychology of God does not differ so much from scientific psychology, as the psychologists' favorite joke points out: How many psychologists does it take to change a light bulb? Only one, but the light bulb has to really want to change.

Change is what it is all about. People go to a psychologist when they recognize the need for a change in their lives and have not been able to bring about this change independently. Change does not come easily. One time back in the day, when I was studying theater, the following discussion question arose among some of my fellow actors, "Why do people go to the theater? What is it that they are ultimately looking for?" Many answers were given, but the answer that we found most convincing was CHANGE. In a movie, play, or virtually in any other form of performing arts, it is the concept of change that the audience finds most appealing. Within a short period, an audience can observe and experience how a character's life changes significantly. We find this inspiring because we have either gone through a similar change or because we want to go through a similar change.

Take Rocky, for example. At the beginning of the story, Rocky is just a guy struggling to make a living from the only thing he knows how to do. His options are limited, and his future is not so bright. But then he gets his big chance, and he seizes the moment. Rocky gets up early, chugs down a few raw eggs, chases some chickens, beats up a side of beef, and a few scenes later, he delivers a fight that changes his life forever. We watch that and become inspired, but if it were only that easy. In reality, change is not nearly so easy to come by, which is why we seek to experience change through our entertainment. When a person is in need of a change, there is no quick fix, easy solution, or storyboard script, which will wrap it all up in two hours.

When I bring my car to the mechanic, he will ask me what is wrong with it. Now, I know nothing at all about cars, but still, I might be able to point in a general direction and say something in it is not running properly, it sounds funny, the tire is flat, or it does not start. Beyond that, I have to say; you are the mechanic. Just take it for a ride, figure out what is wrong, and fix it. In the meantime, I am going to get a cappuccino, call me when you are finished. It may sound somewhat sarcastic, but often people go to a psychologist with a similar attitude. They come in, say something is wrong, but can not say what exactly it is. Then they expect the psychologist to fix it, as one would expect from an auto mechanic.

Bringing about change in a person's life is a much longer and exhausting process than fixing a car because a psychologist cannot simply jump into the heart, body, mind, and soul of a client and take it for a test drive throughout their daily lives. As such, it should not be too surprising that the average success rate for a full psychological recovery is probably only about 30% across the world (Westmacott, 2011). Obviously, scientific psychology does not have all of the answers. With this book, I am attempting to build a bridge between scientific psychology and the psychology of God. To do this, I have taken various aspects of life, such as childhood development, emotional behavior, the human mind, life stress, etc., into consideration and viewed these concepts from both the perspectives of scientific psychology and the psychology of God that is found in the Bible.

Unlike a mechanic who attempts to give tips on fixing a car he has never driven, God does know you, your pain, problems, fears, sorrows, and everything else there is to know about you (Psalm 139:1-24). In fact, he has been riding alongside you the whole time. He has heard the engine, seen the accident, knows exactly what has happened and what is broken; and, He knows what needs to be done to fix it. So let us take a look at the psychology of God.

Of Science and Theology

Although I do openly declare my service to the Lord Jesus Christ, who created the universe and specifically me, I also believe that He created me with a specific purpose: to be a scientist. Thus, in this work, I am proposing to address various psychological constructs from both the perspectives of scientific psychology and Christian theology. I never understood why Christians were sometimes so intimidated and threatened by science. If one believes that God exists, then one should have faith that science will eventually also come to that conclusion, just as it is stated in Luke 12:2, "There is nothing concealed that will not be disclosed, or hidden that will not be made known." Science is a process that is based on the measurement and analysis of quantitative data, in which questions are proposed and evaluated through the scientific method.

As a Christian and a scientist, I am reminded of the passage in the Bible where (doubting) Thomas said, "... unless I see the nail marks in his hands and put my hand into his side, I will not believe" (John 20:25, NIV). This is often depicted as shamefully wrong, suggesting we all need to have blind faith, or we will not be blessed. Rather than debating that issue, I think it is more important to point out that Jesus obliged Thomas and gave him the proof he requested. Only after that did he say, stop doubting and believe (John 20:27, NIV). Similarly, in the absence of Jesus' physical presence here on Earth today, many scientists require more tangible evidence than I do. But I dare say this makes me no less a scientist, and being a scientist makes me no less a Christian. In fact, I would argue that each aspect strengthens the other. Ironically, the three people who have brought me closer to God in the last five years are Richard Dawkins, Lawrence Kraus, and Christopher Hitchens. For it was their animosity toward God that inspired me to consider the psychological evidence for God's existence. To them, I would declare,

"The Father who sent me has himself testified concerning me. You have never heard his voice nor seen his form, nor does his word dwell in you, for you do not believe the one he sent. You study the Scriptures diligently because you think that in them you have eternal life. These are the very Scriptures that testify about me, yet you refuse to come to me to have life" (John 5:37-40). For they study biology, Physics, and Philosophy but fail to recognize that these subjects are also a testimony of God's greatness.

Scientific Method, Data Analysis, and Interpretation

The scientific method is the thought process that human beings have developed and used to solve problems. However, there are a few drawbacks to this method of thinking. Firstly, it is long and tedious. For example, although the Bible has stated that the universe had a definite beginning and will have an ending, science has long believed that the universe simply always existed and always will. Only relatively recently has science come to this same conclusion as the Bible. Secondly, the scientific method can only be used to address falsifiable questions. Science cannot be expected to be used to prove that God (or anything else for that matter) does not exist.

Furthermore, the knowledge gained through the scientific method can only be based upon something else that is already known. That is, science cannot be used to gain an understanding of something that we do not know that we do not know. As such, scientific thinking is based upon a set of knowns or at least assumptions. Before they begin observing data, many scientists make the assumption that God does not exist; however, I do not make this assumption. Upon observing the data without this assumption, it may be easily argued that scientific knowledge does not conflict with Christian theology. While the scientific method is the most effective means of gaining new knowledge, it can only be used to answer the question HOW, but it cannot be used to answer the question WHY. For this reason, science cannot be used to gain new knowledge about God directly. However, it can be used to gain understanding and knowledge of His creation.

For example, it is commonly known that wood floats on water. If I were to ask a scientist why wood floats on water, he/she may very likely respond by stating that the density of wood is less than the density of water; thus, wood floats on water. Okay, but then why do ocean liners, made of metal, being denser than water, float on water. To this, he/she would reply that the volume of water displaced by the ocean liner has a greater mass than the ocean liner itself; thus, the ocean liner floats on water. Okay, but then, why does a paperclip float on water? To this, one could state that when the paperclip is carefully placed on the water, the paperclip's weight is not enough to break the surface tension of the water, even though the paperclip has a greater density and less displacement mass. So, you see, although the scientist's explanations were all true, he/she was not explaining WHY something floats on water, but HOW something floats on water.

When addressing the question of God's existence, one has to be careful and address the question correctly. Many address this question as one would try to figure out how a magician does a magic trick. Before we begin to think about how he may have done the trick, we first know that no real, true, Harry Potter-like-magic is involved. This possibility is removed from the very beginning of the thought process. Having done that, we contemplate, if possibly magnets, very thin strings, secret compartments, misdirection, mirror, blind angles, or any such conceivable element or apparatus might be involved, based on our existing knowledge and understanding. From here, one may form a hypothesis and then test this hypothesis, which may lead to a convincing theory upon successful testing.

Many scientists address the existence of our universe in the same way. They see all of this here and ask themselves how the universe and life came into existence? Some people begin by first eliminating the possibility that God had something to do with it. Their thought process starts with the assumption that there is no God. As such, no data, observation, or interpretation will ever point to God because this option will have been removed before any data, observations, or interpretations took

Introduction

place. When contradictions in data then arise, one is likely to develop a new theory based on old assumptions instead of questioning the assumptions which lead to the contradiction.

The anthropic cosmological principle (ACP) is a perfect example of this. The ACP essentially states that it is statistically impossible that the universe has come into existence perchance. Barrow and Tipler (2009) illustrated that there are simply too many factors that had to be so precisely the way they are so that life could exist as we know it. In fact, the odds that a single gene could spontaneously assemble have been calculated to be somewhere between $4.3 \times 10\text{-}109$ and $1.8 \times 10\text{-}217$. Thus, the chances that the universe and life just happen to come into existence are inconceivably small. This discovery has led many scientists to reconsider their beginning assumptions that there is no God. Nevertheless, many others maintained their original assumption and formulated new theories to compensate for the scientifically calculated fact that the probability that the universe and life, as we know it, have come to be through chance and Darwinian evolution is virtually zero.

Thus, when one does not, as a result of these scientific findings, reject the assumption that there is no God, then one is forced to find an explanation for this data. The theories of Darwinian evolution and the Multiverse have were established to offer an explanation of how all of this came to be without an intelligent designer (Barrow & Tipler, 2009). Since it has been proven that chance alone can not be responsible for life's existence, instead of concluding that there must be one God, who created all of this, many now believe that there must be an infinite number of Universes.

The only way this universe can be as it is, without God the Creator, is if life and the universe evolved from nothing and that there are an infinite number of universes. Some interpret the data to mean, if the odds of our universe coming into existence without God are so infinitely small, this must mean that there are an infinite number of universes. Then, the odds of anything happening in this universe, however improbable, are again conceivable, even likely, when one assumes an unlimited number of universes.

Although it is often said that the scientific method relies on reasoning and logic rather than belief, belief is undeniably a part of the scientific process and an essential one at that. When a scientist approaches a problem, he/she will develop a hypothesis, which is no more than an answer that he/she believes to be true. Moreover, many scientists dedicate their entire lives to the experimentation of a particular hypothesis. They certainly would not do this unless they believed and even hoped they were right, especially if they developed it themselves.

Scientists take measures to guard against scientific bias, which is the term to describe the danger of contaminating data with belief. For this reason, data are viewed with scrutiny in terms of the reliability and validity of the measurements and the methods applied in the evaluation of data. In short, scientists do believe and openly form a hypothesis based on these beliefs. Nevertheless, they should take care not to rest their conclusions upon their beliefs. As such, scientists attempt to base their conclusions on their data. Still, they know that any and all data are inevitably contaminated with an unknown amount of belief. When scientists discuss data results and conclusions, the topics of reliability and validity are thoroughly addressed. However, when the main-stream media reports scientific findings, they are more concerned with reporting a sensational story than scientific knowledge. Thus, in the main-stream media, there is hardly ever any mention of reliability or validity. When we now also have fake news pouring in from all directions, it has become more critical than ever that we learn HOW to think and question, rather than only learning WHAT to think and question.

Regardless of whether you believe that God created you with a specific purpose or you have come into existence through Darwinian evolution, you would still have needed to go through human development and learn about yourself and the world around you. And in doing so, each individual develops a unique mind, based on the sensory integration of perceptions taken from a completely subjective perspective. That is, no one can experience anyone else's experiences. The closest we can get to this is empathy. Empathy, as defined by Carl Rogers (2007, pg. 243), is the ability "to sense the client's private world as if it were your own, but without ever losing the AS IF quality."

Each person develops a unique account of what they desire and has a unique motivation behind that desire or Edesires. Thus, I would argue that each human has a God. That is, everyone has at least one heart's desire, for which they work to fulfill. Be it family, success, riches, love, nature, science, etc., whatever one's reason is for getting up in the morning and doing what they do that is their god. As such, there is really no such thing as atheism, for even atheists live to fulfill their heart's desires in terms of Matthew 6:21: "For where your treasure is, there your heart will be also." Thus, theists and nontheists can and should work together in solving the mysteries of the world. Nevertheless, both still have to guard against contaminating their data, the analysis, and the interpretation with bias.

Lawrence Krauss, a famous evangelical atheist and biologist, once wrote: "A universe without purpose or guidance may seem, for some, to make life itself meaningless. For others, including me, such a universe is invigorating. It makes the fact of our existence even more amazing, and it motivates us to draw meaning from our own actions and to make the most of our brief existence in the sun, simply because we are here, blessed with consciousness and with the opportunity to do so" (Krauss, 2012, pg.181).

Thus it would seem, Krauss and I have the same goal: knowledge and understanding. It is only in our motivation to pursue these goals that we differ significantly. I want to bring people closer to God through science; he wants to separate people from God through science. Still, I would be a fool not to learn from his science just because we differ in theology. Furthermore, having read much of his work, I am reasonably certain that he would agree that science is motivated through the belief that there is nothing concealed that will not be disclosed or hidden that will not be made known (Luke 12:2 NIV).

Scientific Psychology

While other fields of science tend to be black and white, in the field of psychology, almost everything is in the grey. Scientific psychology differs significantly from other areas of science in that it is not very cut and dry. For example, in medicine, a woman is either pregnant or not; one is HIV positive or negative, and heart rhythm is either normal or abnormal. There is no such thing as being slightly pregnant. However, everyone experiences slight degrees of various psychological symptoms, such as anxiety or depression, at some point in their lives. We have all been depressed or anxious at times. We all have our personality flaws or become out of touch with reality at times. And, we are all neurophysiological products of our genes as well as our environment. In short, nobody is perfect.

In psychology, it is much less about whether or not a person has a particular deficit or not, but rather whether this deficit significantly affects the person's life in such a negative way that the problem needs to be addressed. The term 'significant degree' is used to illustrate that a psychological symptom is only a problem when it becomes a problem. Thus, you will notice that I use the word 'significant' very often in this book. And although it sounds extremely redundant, it is necessary to illustrate that scientific psychology is based on the concept of degrees of significance, and nothing is cut and dry, black or white. For this reason, there is no way to study psychology empirically without using statistical mathematics.

I will spare you the burden of the mathematics behind the studies referenced in this book, but I do want to point out that they are indeed there. I have included an extensive reference list for my fellow scholars so that anyone can find and read the original peer-reviewed studies to which I refer throughout this book. It is probably sufficient for all others to understand how statistical degrees of significance are used to learn about human behaviors. So what scientific psychology has done is to measure countless variables of human behavior on many people; in doing so, they have calculated lines of significance and thresholds.

As a general rule of thumb, such lines of significance can be understood like this. Let us say we have here a child who is suspected of having autism. We could collect a bunch of data on this child's behavior and then compare it with the data from other children. By various means, we measure his speech skills, social behavior, and stereotypical behavior because pre-existing data has shown that children with autism generally have difficulties in these three areas. We may find that his social behavior is different but not significantly different, nor does he demonstrate significant stereotypical behaviors. However, if the child's speech skills were to differ significantly from that of other children, then we would have to determine through further testing whether his speech deficiencies could be a result of any other known disorder and rule them out one by one. Eventually, we may be able to conclude with a 95% certainty that the speech problems that child has are indeed associated with a pervasive developmental disorder, i.e., autism. The child could then be diagnosed with autism, which would then be understood as fact; however, only with 95% certainty. What about the remaining 5%? In the remaining 5% lies the truth. Although scientific technology is simply incredible, I mean WOW! the things that we can measure today compared to only 100 years ago; we have come a long way. However, when we compare what we know with what is yet to be known, we may have only scratched the surface. While the scientific method has been used to answer many questions, it has produced significantly more questions than answers.

It is often pointed out that there are more synaptic connections in the human brain than stars in the Milky Way. In the last 100 years, we have made outstanding scientific discoveries. We have discovered that the human brain consists of various parts, each with different cognitive functions. Moreover, the multiple parts often work together to carry our more complex functions, such as speech and social behavior. However, if one were to keep asking deeper 'how' questions, eventually one would have to respond with a humble, we do not know. Moreover, we do not know a fraction of the knowledge that has the potential to become known. And although we have significantly increased our understanding of the human brain, the emotions, mind, and soul greatly remain a mystery.

Through science, we have learned much about ourselves and the universe in which we live we live. And in doing so, we should not fear that our belief in God might be jeopardized. Our belief in God does not reduce our faith in science, which is demonstrated when we travel in an airplane, turn the ignition of a car, or take an aspirin. At the same time, our belief in science should not reduce our faith in God. Therefore, Christians should encourage scientists to do their work, follow it, and learn from it. For even though some scientists are motivated to demonstrate that God has not created the universe and everything in it, so far, all they have come up with are significant reasons to believe.

Amaziah: God is my Strength

Now that I have introduced this book before we can dig into the psychology of God, I feel it is necessary to introduce myself. At a very young age, I was born to one of the physically strongest men in the world, the fourth-strongest, to be exact, at least at one time. In my family, strength was always a fundamental attribute of our lives. Everyone in my family is very proud of their strength, and they all have reason to be. When I was younger, I, too, was very proud of my strength. Wrestling was my passion. Like my father, I loved to test my strength against others. Being the strongest, the fastest, and above all else, the hardest working was more important to me than winning. Because of this, I never lost a match. However, occasionally, I did run out of time while the score was not yet in my favor or got pinned before I could pin my opponent. However, my story does not end with an Olympic gold medal, as was my goal back then. My athletic career ended with a series of injuries that probably were ultimately caused by muscular dystrophy (MD). However, I did not know that until much later.

Nevertheless, the strength in my muscles began to leak like a faucet. Everything that I had strived for, up until that point in my life, had now become unreachable. So, I went to college for academics instead of sports. I was pretty good at math and found chemistry interesting, so I started out studying chemical engineering at Ohio University in Athens, Ohio. I tried to put the same discipline into my studies that I had before in wrestling. But, something was missing: the passion. It was at this time that I met some students on the campus greens who were juggling. Instantly, I found my new passion. I had already been able to juggle three balls. However, I picked up the fourth ball on this day, and soon after, I had the fifth in my hand. I juggled every day. It was not long after that I began skipping my chemical engineering classes to juggle and sit in on dance, acting, and music classes. Mind you, at this point; I still did not know that I had MD. Despite my newfound passion for the performing arts, I managed to graduate from Ohio University with a bachelor's degree in math.

Directly after I received my diploma, I took off for Germany to spend a summer working as a street performer at the various wine festivals throughout the Rhein-Main area. Once again, having learned what it meant to work hard and to give one's best in everything one does, I practiced juggling and other circus skills with as much or even more diligence as ever. This hard training made me finally face up to the fact that my right arm was getting weaker and weaker. My attempt to build back the strength in my right arm only reduced it to a twig.

Finally, I went to the doctor. I noticed immediately that the doctors took the smallness of my right arm very seriously and said I would have to stay a few days to run some tests. I protested and said that I had a show to do that night. The doctor, who was quite unfriendly, simply replied that I might not be doing any more shows if this was not looked into immediately. Scare tactics, I thought. They just want to run up a high bill. That is what happens when you live in a country with universal health care. So, the doctor brought me to what seemed to be a refrigerated table, told me to strip to my underwear, and lay on the refrigerated table.

Then about 15 medical students came in, and from that point on, the doctor only addressed them and referred to me as "the patient," as he demonstrated how to perform a nerve conduction scan. A nerve conduction scan tests, as the name implies, the electric conductivity of the nerves. This is what they do. They put a metal ring around your wrist, and then they stick a very tiny pin into a nerve and measure the distance between the pin and the metal ring. How do they know when they have the pin in the nerve, you ask? Well, it is not in and out like a shot. They stick the pin in your arm and fish around with it a bit, and they know they have it in the nerve when the patient screams. Then they say relax; they do not want to have any confounding neuro activity going on. And when they think you are relaxed enough, they hit a button and zap you with an electrical shock right into the nerve. They want to know how many volts they need to get the current up to a certain speed. So they start with a lower voltage and repeat the procedure again and again, upping the voltage each time until they reach the desired speed. I was shocked about 80 times in both arms and legs by a bunch of medical students, while I was made to lay on a refrigerated table wearing only a paper gown as the doctor looked on. A very horrible experience, but the worse thing about it was that they would tell me to relax before each shock while moving their hand toward the shock button. Compared to that, the muscle biopsy was easy.

I went head to head with the doc and the staff after this horrible experience. I did not want to be there, and so I made sure that they did not want me there either. But, I was told I had to stay until the test results came back. When they did, the doctor came up to my bed and said, "Mr. Kolb, you have Emory Dryfuss Syndrome; here is a brochure about it, and this one is from the MDA; you should contact them." Then he moved on to the next patient, which was the last time I saw or talked to this doctor. As I was getting dressed to go home, I started reading the first few lines of the brochure. It read something like this, 'Emory Dryfuss syndrome is a chronic and progressive muscle disease that usually leads to death in two years. ...' That is as far as a got, and then

I began ringing for the nurse. What is this? Are you guys telling me I am going to die in two years?! And this is the way you tell me?! Needless to say; I flipped out a bit.

Life was going so well. I was making good money by doing what I would have gladly done for free. Traveling all over Germany and even Europe doing street shows, learning languages, people, and places, but once again, my dreams and goals were shattered. I was ultimately becoming that, for which I had no respect: weakness. I hate weakness. And I hate fear. And I hate cowardliness. I realized that I had only two options. The first one is not even worth mentioning because giving up is never an option. So, I had to become strong again, stronger than I was when I measured strength in pounds or repetitions. I needed to find the kind of strength that enables one to put themselves on the line every day, day for day. So, what happened then? I became a clinic clown. A strength, which has nothing to do with muscle, came out of me through my work as a clown.

It just so happened that at that time, I was working with a group of clowns who had been inspired by the movie Patch Adams. We were the first group of clowns to perform as Clown Doctors in Germany. Now there are clown doctors in many children's hospitals worldwide (Doehring & Renz, 2003). I had been using humor to help children cope with various serious ailments, and now it was time that I practiced what I preached. Thus, I dove into humor, my new passion, with all my heart, body, mind, and soul. I had heard the saying, "you can either die with an illness or live with an illness," and had said it many times myself. But now, I was in the perfect position to demonstrate that it is much better to live with an illness than to die with the illness.

The strength in my arms, shoulders, and back ran out like the sand in an hourglass, but I did not die. Either a miracle occurred, or the doctors misdiagnosed me. Either way, now it seems as though I have FSH MD, a form that only robs the body of all its strength very slowly but does not kill it. The great thing about clowning is that it turns deficits into attributes. A person, who cannot talk, can play a clown that does not talk, a person who cannot walk can play a clown who does not walk; and a person, who cannot sit still, can play a clown that does not sit still. So, just as 2 Corinthians 12:9 states, my power was made perfect in my weakness. I developed a clown character, Dr. Clou, whose behaviors and attributes were defined and motivated by the symptoms of MD, but who was otherwise perfectly healthy. Indeed, I felt much better after having worked a day in my clown character than I did before that day's work. It was on my days off, in which the MD was quite troubling.

Since laughter and humor are said to be the best medicine, I decided to treat it as such and study humor. Which forms of humor should be prescribed for which ailments, and at what dosage, and how should it be administered? In 2005 I began the transition from clinic clown to a licensed psychologist. During my master's studies in clinical and counseling psychology, I focused on the concept of humor. This inspired me to work with children with developmental disorders and their parents. This work became my new passion, and my performing arts skills came to very good use. I would say only about 20% of my therapeutic method was derived from what I learned as a psychology student, and 80% was based on my experience as a clown and performing artist. However, eventually, the MD, once again, got so bad and severely affected the strength in my legs that I could no longer work with this clientele effectively and productively.

Therefore, having recognized the therapeutic potential of various aspects of the performing arts in the field of psychology, I was determined to investigate this more in-depth. Thus, I continued with my academic studies and obtained my Ph.D. in general psychology. I studied and researched emotional processing from both the perspectives of scientific psychology and theatrical arts. Both the fields of scientific psychology and theatrical arts are dedicated to the study of human behavior. And although they differ in their motivation and study technique, these two professional fields have much to offer the other. Thus, I made it a goal to build a bridge between them, which I accomplished with the completion of my dissertation: Directed expression: Quantifying emotional expression with concepts derived from the performing arts.

During all this time, MD has impacted my personal life as much if not more than it has my professional life. My marriage eventually broke due to the stress associated with living and loving someone with a progressive and chronic illness. I cannot imagine how hard it must be to watch a loved one slowly deteriorate over time, but it was simply too much for my ex-wife. My three children have practically been raised by three different forms of me with different levels of strength. My oldest daughter, I was still able to hold in my good arm as she was a baby, and I went jogging with her every day. Ten years later, I became a father again. By then, my arms were so weak that I could not carry or lift my own child. Five years later, my third child was born, who is now five, and I wonder if she will have any memories of me walking. Come what may, Romans 8:28 has carried me through all of this; and, each and every one of my problems has turned out for the good. Although I have often been told that I should simply curse God and die, I thank Him and praise Him for His Faithfulness and Grace, and for the strength I have in my fingers to type and to build more bridges – bridges between Christianity and science, and between psychology and theology. Herein lies the meaning of life and the key to happiness, to strive to fulfill God's purpose in our lives. God created each of us with a specific purpose. If we do our best to find and fulfill this purpose, then come what may, sickness or storm, we will always be happy and content.

Focus: A Philosophical Perspective

I once had a fascinating discussion with a very bright young man. In the course of our discussion, I had told him much about my life and the obstacles I had overcome with God's help. He then asked me if I could prove it was God's help and then asserted that a feeling was no proof. He suggested that by merely having such a strong focus in my life, I have better-overcome trials and tribulations than if I had no focus in life regardless of the focus. That is, it was not God that was helping me, but it was me helping myself through my core belief in God.

I had to admit that this was a thought-provoking idea that may be explained through psychology. He was suggesting that God works essentially on the Placebo Effect. This concept asserts that it is not God that helps one navigate life, but merely the strong belief in a god gives one the strength to overcome difficulties. It was then that I realized that in one point, he was right and that there is no such thing as atheism because everyone is a slave to their god, whatever that may be. For some, it is money for others power, but it could also be their children or goodness or even love itself. That which our hearts desire most is what we live for, and that is our god. And if you say, "I don't live for anything but for me in the here and now." Then you are your own god (Mat 6:21).

This brings us back to the Old Testament challenge, which is the true God. Is it only a placebo effect, or is there a God that leads me through my trials and tribulations? I believe there is a God, Creator of Heaven and Earth, that leads me through my trial and tribulations, but how can I prove it? Most Christians will say, "I just know it" or "I can feel it." However, for this young man, that was no evidence. He wanted something he could see and touch. He needed a reason to believe. Hugh Ross, an astrophysicist, offers many reasons to believe from his field, but what evidence can the field of scientific psychology bring forth?

I told him that if my God was not the one and only true God of the universe and if all of this were not true, then I would not be content as I am, with that what I have. I have gone through a lot of shit, just like other people, but one difference is that I am thankful for the shit I have had to endure because it has helped me to become the person whom God created me to become. God did not make human-beings but rather human-becomings. God is not so terribly interested in who we are now and even less interested in who we were in the past; God is interested in whom we are becoming.

If you take a look at other people who follow other gods, such as money, power, fun, sex, etc., the one big difference is contentment. In the field of scientific psychology, this is commonly referred to as life satisfaction. Scientific psychology has painstakingly attempted to define, measure, and research the concept of life satisfaction. Martikainen (2009) pointed out that research on life satisfaction could also fall within the domains of philosophy, sociology, economics, or public health. It has been a subject of great interest and importance since Aristotle's Nicomachean ethics in 350 BC. While Martikainen adopted Veenhoven's (1991) definition of life satisfaction as the degree to which an individual judges the overall quality of their life as a whole, he also pointed out that various researchers have used various definitions, depending on which aspects of life satisfaction they intended to focus. For example, Diener and Lucas (1999) argued that one's life satisfaction is closely related to optimism but failed to determine whether life satisfaction leads to optimism or if optimism leads to life satisfaction. Veenhoven (1996) pointed out that different factors related to the concept of life satisfaction include economic well-being, social equality, and political freedom. These authors also discovered that individuals who came from a similar domain still had significantly different life satisfaction perceptions. As such, it certainly cannot be stated that one's life satisfaction is more closely associated with any specific area of life, such as one's economic well-being, social equality, or political freedom.

On the other hand, some distinct patterns have been established. For example, young adults and adolescents, in particular females, have been found to be significantly less satisfied with their lives than children and adults (Moksnes & Espnes, 2013; Burger & Samuel, 2017). As such, it would seem no matter how the concept of life satisfaction is perceived, it is always viewed or measured in terms of dependent factors, in relation to other factors, but never on its own, independent from any other factors at all. Also, one may have thought that if one's life satisfaction is dependent on many various domains, then an increase in one domain could allow for a decrease in another domain; however, Rojas (2006) found that this is generally not the case. That is, when it comes to one's satisfaction with one's life, the whole is not equal to the sum of its parts. Rojas examined this even further and discovered that life satisfaction is not only a purely subjective construct, and no single domain could replace any other fully and completely. Even studies conducted on various health problems demonstrated that poor health did not equate directly with poor life satisfaction, and good health did not directly correspond with good life satisfaction. The only possible single determinant in a specific age group that did seem to have a direct and causal relationship with life satisfaction was the level of one's perceived cognitive ability in old age (Rabbit et al., 2007).

Thus, it would seem that by scientific means, researchers have not been able to find the key to happiness. It seems to be a very complex problem with an unknown number of variables that are yet to be set into a viable equation. Someone who longs for power will never have enough power, someone who longs for money will never have enough money, and someone who longs for love will never feel loved enough, and so on. Furthermore, such individuals will live in constant fear of losing what they have. However, those who long to follow God's will and become the person he has created them to become will be satisfied in all other matters. Followers of God do not have to live in constant fear of losing what they have. Regardless of disease, divorce, pain, suffering, whatever may come, all trials and tribulations simply become scenes where one can see God, up close and personal, working in our lives.

Moreover, when God becomes your heart's greatest desire, and you learn to trust in him fully, you will begin to greet and even take pleasure in your trials and tribulations because that is when you can see God working actively and directly in your life. When I was younger, I thought that Romans 5:3–5 was to be taken metaphorically:

> "We also glory in our sufferings, because we know suffering brings perseverance; perseverance, character; and character, hope. And hope does not put us to shame, because God's love has been poured out into our hearts through the Holy Spirit, who has been given to us."

Introduction

So finally, the ultimate proof that God is real and He guides us through our trials and tribulations is us, His followers, the people who live fearlessly, generously, and consider themselves already dead to this world. When I tell people this, they think I am nuts, but the second greatest gift (after salvation) that I have ever received from God, is my death to this world. After the doctors told me I had only two years to live, I thought, okay, I will live these last two years for God and only for God. I will be unreservedly obedient to the Holy Spirit, and I will give my life to God, not metaphorically but literally. I was able to do this because I thought I only had two years left anyway. So from that point on, I concentrated on receiving impulses from the Holy Spirit. If I felt an urge to turn left instead of right, I did so. If I felt the urge to go up to someone and talk to them, I did so. Every impulse I received, I followed. And then the most amazing things began to happen. God began using me every day and in the most incredible ways. I traveled through Europe doing street shows and witnessing to people, helping people, and living an incredibly blessed life while expecting to die.

Obviously, I did not die. So, what happened? I do not know. I certainly still have some sort of MD, but my heart is still beating, and I am still breathing. But none of that concerns me at all anymore because I have already died in this world, and I am already living in the next. When people decide to accept Jesus in their hearts, they often do so to have eternal life and go to heaven when they die. While this is true, it is not entirely true. Salvation does not begin after one becomes old and dies; salvation begins in this life. When we accept Jesus into our hearts as our Lord and Savior, we are not supposed to put our lives into his hands metaphorically. Instead, we are to consider ourselves dead to this world literally. Our heart, body, and mind die, but it is our soul that will be judged before God, and through which we become a new creation.

When you do this and die to this world, you will know what I mean because you will have no more fear, no more sorrow, no more anxiety, or depression. Nothing will ever be able to harm you, hurt you, or negatively affect you. When problems arise, you will rejoice and face them with excitement and say that this will be great. I am about to see God working in my life again. I am not saying you are not going to have any more problems. In fact, you will have more. When you begin living like this, you become a target for the devil; he does not want people living like this. It is very bad for his business. People who are dead to this world become a light in the darkness, attracting other people who also want to overcome their fears. So, the devil will attack you and those around you, and particularly those that you love, in a desperate attempt to get you to go back to your old life.

Therefore, if you are right now thinking about giving up your life in this world, and giving your life to Christ and dying to this world, do not make this decision lightly. Please know that you will lose everything you have in this world. This is not an altar call. No one will applaud you. No one will tell you how courageous you are. No one will be happy for you and welcome you to the Kingdom of God. People, even people from your church, will think you have lost your mind. They will think you are delusional. They will hate you for no longer caring or being concerned about matters of this world. Nothing that you treasured before, not your wife, not your children, not your job, money, or even your well-being, will be of any importance to you. All you will be is a single light shining in the darkness, empowered through the Holy Spirit; and, that will be the only thing that matters to you.

Nature versus Nurture: Are we only a product of our DNA?

As I started writing this book, I was not sure for whom I was writing it. For a while, I thought it might be a book about the existence of God. The fields of Physics and Biology generate much debate on the existence of God. However, evidence from the field of psychology has been greatly ignored. In my psychological research, I have come across a lot of information about DNA and its influence on behavior and development. However, previously I asserted that one should allow the Holy Spirit to guide one's behaviors and foster one's character development. But is that not a direct contradiction to the scientific findings of psychological research? Has not psychology determined that one's behavior and character development is predetermined in one's DNA? Many studies, especially those cited in popular rather than academic media, would defend this position.

This question has become known as the Nature versus Nurture debate. The Nature side of the issue claims that who we are and whom we will become is predetermined in our DNA at the moment of conception, and there is little we can do to change that. The Nurture side of the issue claims that it is the experiences of our surroundings that determine who we are and whom we will become. Like all good debates, there is empirical evidence, which supports both sides of the issue. This is my take on the question of nature versus nurture.

Many psychologists have argued that genetics play a much larger role in influencing human behavior than originally believed (Broderick & Blewitt, 2006; O'Connor, 2006; Plomain, Reiss, Hetherington, & Howe, 1994). It remains clear that both our DNA and our environment influence human behavior, but to what extent? Behavior genetics rely on the assumption that the genetic influence on behavior can be separated from environmental influences. This is done by conducting behavioral studies on identical twins who have been separated at birth and comparing this to adopted children living in the same environment. Many such studies have been conducted in which various behavioral measurements have been taken and compared in various combinations of identical, fraternal twins and adopted children under the conditions of living in the same environment and different environments.

It has been found that identical twins demonstrate significantly more similar behaviors when compared to other children living in the same environment (Broderick & Blewitt, 2006; O'Connoer, 2006; Plomain et al., 1994). These results suggest that our DNA may have significantly more influence on our development than our environment. I can understand why many find such research important because parents of children with developmental disorders often are plagued with the question, why? Why is my child like this? What went wrong? Is it something I did wrong, or did someone else do something? Who or what is to blame for this problem? When working with parents in this situation, I encourage them not to get hung up on this question. Just because the results of a scientific study are significant does not mean the science is significant. Until we have the ability to alter DNA effectively and productively, it does not matter if the problems are of genetic origin or not, the cards have been dealt, and that is simply the hand that has to be played.

This may sound brutally honest, especially to parents of children with a developmental disorder due to a gene defect. However, the danger I am trying to avoid is the apathetic compliance of merely accepting the problem and saying, "Well, we cannot do anything about it, so we will not do anything about it." Let me remind you; I am not only speaking as a doctor of psychology but as a person with a genetic disorder, whose three biological children each have a 50% chance of acquiring FSH MD. Still, I knowingly chose to have biological children. Why? Because I live a completely fulfilled life, and I can teach them how to do the same. Furthermore, when it comes to coping with and counteracting behavioral and developmental problems, I could argue that a child's environment has significantly more influence on his/her behavior and development than his DNA.

At the point of conception, the entire influence of DNA has come and gone. After that point, there is no other significant change expected in the DNA. As I said before, at the moment of conception, the cards are dealt, and one has to play those cards, with no exchanges and no wild cards. Moreover, when we look at the cards, that is, the DNA genes, the number of different hands that can be dealt is astronomically large but is nevertheless mathematically limited. There is not an infinite number of possible DNA combinations that could be put together, resulting in a human being. As such, our behavior and character development's genetic influence is a limited to a one-time event.

On the other hand, from conception until death, the environment continually influences our development and behavior (Zuckerman, 1999). During this time, virtually every moment of each day, there are an infinite number of things that happen and an infinite number of things that do not happen. Each of these may have a significant influence on the course of our behavior and development. Therefore, the co-action of the various developmental processes should not be disregarded. Kolb (2008) attempted to illustrate the importance of considering the co-action between each of the developmental processes. The attachment theory, physical development, moral development, social development, cognitive development, identity development, interpersonal relationships, gender, culture, vocational development, emotional development, and all other thinkable developmental processes have all been found to be significantly influenced by our environment. Furthermore, while there is nothing that we can do about our DNA, humans are unique in that they can and do change their environment and behavior. Thus, instead of surrendering to our DNA, we should view a problem as previously defined: a problem is something with a solution.

A problem is something with a solution. If it does not have a solution, then it is not a problem, but rather a fact. Problems can be solved, but facts have to be accepted. Life stress, depression, anxiety, and other mental illnesses can arise when individuals accept problems as facts or when they try to solve facts as if they were problems. Thus, discerning the difference between problems and facts is the first step toward mental, emotional, and physical well-being. The process is quite simple. When confronted with something that worries you, break it down into facts and problems. Allow me to use myself as an example. I have FSH MD, problem, or fact? Fact. FSH MD is chronic and progressive. There is no cure or therapy. Many people spend their lives searching for one, but they miss out on living life to the fullest in the process. I am not referring to the scientists trying to develop a cure for incurable diseases, but rather diseased people, who spend all their time searching for and trying one alleged remedy after another.

On the other hand, I cannot walk very well or far. That is not a fact but merely a problem. The solution is a wheelchair. You will hopefully never have to understand how much wheelchairs suck. Many people would rather accept it as a fact that they cannot walk than to accept this solution. These people just give up living and turn into hermits because they accept a problem as a fact.

Instead of inadvertently trying to solve a fact or simply accepting a problem, it is vital to recognize the difference between a problem and a fact. In order to break down FSH MD into facts and problems, I first considered the things about the FSH MD that can be solved. FSH MD is coupled with chronic pain. Fact or problem? Problem! There are more than enough pain meds out there that one can use. FSH MD causes extreme weakness and fatigue, Problem or Fact? This one is a bit more difficult because the wording is crucial. The wording expresses the perspective, but this is a fact; FSH MD causes extreme fatigue and weakness. I cannot hold objects that are more than a pound for any significant length of time. Even a large cappuccino from McDonald's is too heavy.

Nevertheless, that is a problem rather than a fact because I can just order a small cappuccino in a to-go cup, which is much lighter. There are many things that I am simply incapable of doing. This is not a fact, but merely a problem, because now I have learned to swallow my pride and ask people to help me with things I cannot do for myself. I could continue like this over many aspects of my life with FSH MD, but I think you get the point. My DNA has caused me to have FSH MD, but FSH MD or my DNA has not determined who I am and whom I will become.

My environment has had a much greater impact on my life than my wretched DNA. It was my father who taught me to never give up. It was my mother who taught me how to communicate and speak my mind rationally rather than emotionally. Growing up on a farm during my childhood taught me the beauty and wonder of nature. My high school girlfriend taught me that love in a friendship is no less valuable than love in a romantic relationship. I have learned who I am and who I am not through my experiences and not through my DNA. Therefore, in the debate between nature and nurture, I argue that nurture wins by default because nature (DNA) is merely a fact that has to be accepted. Nevertheless, it is how we deal with the problems we face in life that make us who we are and who we will become. It is not the problems we face but how we face our problems that matter.

CHAPTER TWO

The Four Components of the Human: Heart, Body, Mind, and Soul

When Jesus said, "Love the Lord your God with all of your heart and with all your soul and with all your mind and with all your strength" (Mark 12:30, NIV), He was emphasizing that one should love the Lord completely with one's entire being. Moreover, we should love God with each of these four parts distinctly. The love we project with each of these four parts is significantly different from the others. To put it briefly, loving God with all of our heart means to love Him, and thus also others, compassionately, to the point that our heart groans to the point that it can no longer express our feelings (Romans 8:26). Loving God and others with all of our minds means to do so with full concentration. A percentage of the children brought to me for evaluation are brought because their parents or teachers suspected that the child has a concentration problem. In this case, the first question I ask is: does the child watch TV? "Yes, he can watch TV all day." Well, then he does not have a concentration problem; he has a motivation problem. A concentration problem means a person is unable to focus on anything for a significant amount of time, even if he wants to. However, in most cases, a person can concentrate on things of great interest for a very long time, but not on things of lesser interest, like studying. Thus, to love with all of our minds means first, that love becomes our greatest interest. And secondly, that we discipline our minds always to be focused on the love of God, always and forever. To love with all of our strength also requires a great deal of discipline and strict training. In 1. Corinthians 9: 24-27, Paul compares what it means to love God with all of our strength to the training of an elite athlete, and then some. Having grown up the son of a professional football player for the Pittsburgh Steelers, who won 4 Superbowls in 5 years, I have learned what it means to make one's body one slave, as Paul describes. It means to push it far beyond what you think it can do. Finally, to love God with all of the soul means to strive for righteousness. In our struggle against sin, Paul tells us that we should resist it to the point of bleeding (Hebrews 12:4). Again, that seems very extreme, but nevertheless, that is what it means to love with all of our souls. It means doing what one knows to be right and good, all the time, 24/7 (James 4: 17). These are, of course, all unattainable goals, for man is simply sinful. Nevertheless, these are the goals for which we should strive. In Romans 7: 15-25, Paul describes his war against sin and concludes that this is a struggle that we will face all of our lives, but through the blood of Jesus, we will eventually win, so long as we keep striving for righteousness.

The fact that Matthew 22:37 only mentions the heart, soul, and mind, while Luke 10:27 only mentions the heart, soul, and strength, illustrates how confusing these components can be and how difficult it can be to isolate these individual components from each other. Before I continue, let me briefly insert the component of strength is referring to physical strength and not mental or emotional strength. As such, the components labeled 'strength' may more broadly be referred to as the body and will be labeled as such from here on.

Throughout the Bible, one can find references to the heart, body, mind, and soul in various combinations or individually. For example, my Bible notes that Jesus is referring to Deuteronomy, which speaks only of the heart, soul, and body. One of my favorite Bible verses is Colossians 3:2-3, "...set your hearts on things above ... set your mind on things above," pointing out that the heart and the mind can do the same thing but independently from each other. I would not expect that many would disagree that it is certainly possible to do something with great passion, but with little concentration, or do something with great concentration but with little passion. And it should follow logically that maximum concentration and passion are likely to yield better results than either concentration or passion alone. Scientific psychology has found that doing something with concentration but without passion may lead to what we now call burnout (Bakker, Demerouti, & Sanz-Vergel, 2014).

Many, if not perhaps even all, passages that refer to the heart, body, mind, or soul seem to be directly associated with scientific psychology findings. For example, Proverbs 4:23, "Above all else, guard your heart, for everything you do flows from it" (NIV). This verse points out what scientific psychology has come to understand. When our emotional processing system kicks in, and an emotional episode begins, the autonomic nervous system (ANS) takes over, and the central nervous system (CNS) loses control (Harris & Katkin, 1975; Lazarus, 1991; Barnard et al., 2007). At this moment, an emotional episode is initiated, and we become "emotional." It is impossible to become aware of this moment of the initiation of an emotional episode. We can only become aware that an emotional episode has begun after the fact because when we become emotional, our level of conscious awareness falls significantly. Paul Ekman's discovery of micro-expression, extremely fast, and uncontrollable emotional facial expressions are an example of this (Ekman, 2003).

For this reason, interrogators are trained to pay particularly close attention to specific facial muscles that are significantly more directly controlled by the ANS rather than the CNS. Thus, when we lie, the emotional stress involved causes inadvertent bodily behaviors. Even when one tries to suppress the known behavioral indications of lying, other behaviors commonly referred to as seepage (or leakage) surfaces elsewhere. As such, Navarro (2008) suggested that attached to every good poker face is a twitching foot or something under the table.

The only way to significantly avoid seepage is by involving the soul and the mind in the conflict between the heart and the body. It is this internal conflict between these four human components that causes emotional seepage. For example, a confabulation refers to a lie about which the mind and soul have come to believe as true. This can happen when a person lives a lie for a significant amount of time. When this happens, the mind and soul accept the lie as truth, and the body no longer reacts stressfully. For example, individuals with Schizophrenia, in which one exhibits the clinical symptom of some sort of fracture with respect to one or more aspects of reality, may not show any abnormalities on a lie detector test or demonstrate any seepage, as they claim to be Cesar Augustus or the like.

Similarly, the clinical symptoms of psychopathic disorders are characterized by a significant lack of apathy and moral. Such individuals may show no significant indications of lying, because to them, lying is simply a means of getting what they want. Thus, they have no conflict between their heart, body, mind, or soul when they lie, cheat, deceive, or harm others in any way (Klaver et al., 2007, 2009).

Thus, a psychologist's primary goal is to help clients find a balance and resolve conflicts between their hearts, bodies, minds, and souls. Furthermore, practically all psychopathological disorders listed and described in the various diagnostic manuals may be summarized or defined as conflicts between these four components to varying degrees and combinations. Therefore, it is of great psychological interest to understand how these four components work individually and integrally. For in order to figure out what can be done about a psychological disorder, one has to break it down in terms of heart, body, mind, and soul. Furthermore, it is of great theological interest to compare the Bible's understanding of the function of these components to that of scientific psychology.

In the therapy of psychological disorders, one may first begin with one of the four components and work from there towards the other components. Indeed each of the many various therapeutic methods could be described as starting with one of the four components and from there reaching out toward the others until they are all in sync with each other. After about 150 years, scientific psychology has come to understand that the human being is made up of heart, body, mind, and soul, just as Jesus said. Therefore, if we now know that the body is made up of these four components, and the field of therapeutic psychology is essentially the effort of getting these components in sync with each other, perhaps the best way to do that is to have each of the four components focus on the same thing. For it makes sense to me, as a psychologist and as a person struggling with life stress, that if I focus on loving God with all my heart, body, mind, and soul, then each of these components will be in good relation with the other three.

As such, one can easily conclude that the human being is made up of these four intricately integrated components. Interestingly, scientific psychology has come to the same conclusion. Much research has been focused on defining each of these components individually and studying how each of these four components reacts and influences the others. On this matter, psychologists seem to take one of two perspectives: holism and atomism. Atomism is the belief that the whole is the sum of the parts; while, holism is the belief that the whole is greater than the sum of the parts. Holistic therapeutic interventions consider the heart, body, mind, and soul, even when the symptoms seem to be related to only one of these components. Atomistic therapeutic interventions tend to focus primarily on the component from which the symptoms arise. Much is to be said and has been said from both perspectives. But here, I will only point out that the two perspectives exist and that I favor the holistic approach.

Before I continue, I can imagine that many of my readers are now thinking, "What about the spirit?" Others would equate the spirit with the soul. At this point, I want to assure you, I did not forget the spirit, but also point out the spirit is not the same as the soul, but I will expand on that later. For now, let's focus first only on the heart, which is the emotions, the body, which is the biological tissue, the mind, which is our conscious self-awareness, and the soul, which is our sub-conscious self-awareness.

The Four Components of the Human: Heart, Body, Mind, and Soul

Now that we have briefly defined each of these components let's briefly discuss what these components do before we address each component individually in more detail. From each of these four components come impulses, which initiate our behavior; and, each of these four sources delivers a different kind of impulse that affects behavior differently. As such, an impulse is something that sparks the initiation of behavior. This is grounded on the principle that behavior is not random. There is a reason for every action that we make, even though we may not be consciously aware of this reason. Regardless of how incidental it may seem, every movement that we make is somehow somewhere initiated for a reason. A discussion about the possible reasons for any seemingly incidental behavior often does little good and sometimes does considerable harm. If my clients knew why they do what they do, they would probably not need to seek out my help in the first place. Therefore, it is pointless, at best, for anyone to ask why someone behaves the way they do, although much of the goal is to figure out why.

Nevertheless, this goal has to be sought out by other means. Therefore, instead of asking why we have the impulses to behave as we do, it may be more productive to discuss their impulses and where they come from. In doing so, the 'why' may be dredged up.

As previously stated, these four components do not function independently from each other, but rather they are so deeply integrated into each other that science has had great difficulty in gaining information about them independently. Impulses out of each of these four sources can lead to behaviors that generate more impulses from the other three sources. For example, an impulse out of the body, as insignificant as a small stone in a shoe, could lead to a different walk. This different walk, be it faster, or slower, or different in any way at all, will inevitably affect one's emotions. This, in turn, may have a significant influence on one's thoughts, which in turn may again influence the body and the heart.

Moreover, with a significant amount of time, all of this will influence the soul, as impulses for each of these components trigger impulses of other components. All of this happens outside of one's conscious awareness. For example, let's say you are walking by a display case, and you see something that catches your eye. This sensory input may trigger an impulse to go into the store and buy the item; however, the input source will most probably not be limited to only one of the four impulse components exclusively. One may have an idea like, "this would go great with my..." And the sight of the object may trigger an emotional response as simple and subtle as a casual smile. A bodily response, such as stepping out of someone's way, may get your feet stepping towards the door before you are even thought about going in or not. Or an old lady needing help opening the door to the store may give your body the impulse to open the door for her. At which point, you might then think, "Well, I am practically in the store now, so I might as well take a look." And then you perceive this or that, and one impulse leads to an action and this to another, and so on and so forth. And before you know it, you've bought something that 15 minutes ago you neither wanted nor needed. And throughout this process, you were not even consciously aware of the big red 50% off sale sign in the window, nor of any of the other processes going on within your heart, body, mind, and soul that may have significantly contributed to your behaviors without you being consciously aware of it.

As such, all of these impulses work together and lead to implemented behaviors to fulfill our needs, wants, and desires. Thus each component affects and is affected by each other component continually. Now that we have discussed how all of these components work together and serve as sources of behavioral impulses will now be discussed individually. Of these four, the body is the easiest to identify and isolate. Therefore we will begin with the body.

The Body

With the term body, I am referring to the living tissues of the flesh. The body is made up of bones, muscles, nerves, ligaments, tendons, and other such materials that are again made up of living cell tissue. As such, the brain is part of the body, distinct from the mind, which is not made up of living tissue. The mind and the brain are intricately related, and one could not have one without the other. To put it simply, the mind is essentially the abstract and intangible iCloud of the fleshy hard drive brain. As such, Neurophysiology has identified the various parts of the brain, each performing different functions, but there is no single part or parts in which the mind is located. We know where vision, hearing, and various thought processes are computed, but concepts such as understanding, judgment, insight, and wisdom exceed the scope of brain matter and exist only in mind, not the brain.

In some cases, it would seem that the body has a mind of its own. And in a way, it does. In some situations, we don't have time to think about our behavior; the impulse comes directly out of the body. Sport situations are a good example of this. In 'American' football, the players huddle up to talk and think about what they are going to do. But after the ball is snapped, there is no time to think and no time to communicate. If a long pass was planned, but the defense blitz comes too fast, then the tight end doesn't have time to think about looking back at his QB, wondering if he might need an extra receiver. By the time he would think about that, his QB would be sacked.

Similarly, a boxer has no time to realize or think about the right time to throw a punch. Instead, the boxer is in body impulse modus, knowing that it is already too late when he sees an opportunity to strike a blow. The body reacts independently from the mind, much like a reflex.

Sports scientists have identified that it takes the body 0.8 seconds to develop maximum force. The issue in the two examples illustrated above is that in an eighth of a second, your QB is sacked, or your opponent has countered in some significant way. Therefore, impulse, in impact sports, is defined as how much force can be generated in .1 - .2 second or impulse = force x time. If one only trains maximum force (bench press or squats) in practice, the athlete will be unlikely to react appropriately in the "heat" of competition. How intriguing that our physical and mental impulses can cause problems if not prepared through proper training.

Our bodies do so many things, of which we are not aware. As such, we often follow impulses out of the body non-consciously. For example, if a person has a low status, which is projected through his mimic, gestures, postures, and actions, these factors are known to significantly affect what we think and feel. Studies have shown that our bodies influence our minds and emotions (Kepner, 2005; Damasio, 2000, 2003, 2006). This has long since been accepted as true and is often referred to as biofeedback (Lazarus, 1975; Beigle, 1951). We also know that when one becomes emotional, one's thoughts are significantly influenced and vice versa. Take, for example, someone who has bad posture while sitting at the desk at work. This bad posture will then inevitably lead to discomfort, if not pain, in the physiological structure of this person. They will instinctively adapt to this discomfort through some physiological adaptive behavior, which leads to a specific status. It is then from this position that all incoming EPS are then evaluated. As such, bad posture may have a significant effect on the outcomes of these evaluations. This is commonly known as irritability.

Our bodies are perhaps the most vulnerable part of our being. While one may have emotional and mental strength and a flourishing soul throughout their lives until the day they die, everyone has a body that will eventually and undoubtedly deteriorate over time. In addition to this, sin is most deeply rooted in the body, and from there, it infects the heart, mind, and soul. This is true from both psychological and theological perspectives. Psychology is the study of human behavior, and where there is no body, there is no behavior, for behavior is carried out and occurs in and through the body. Even when one focuses on purely mental activity that cannot be expressed in terms of behavior, such as dreams, voices in one's head, thoughts, ideas, and other such abstract mental components, one must concede that none of these mental activities can take place without a brain, which is made up of living tissue and thus belongs to the body. From a theological standpoint, the Bible clearly states that our sinful nature is a result of and lies in our flesh (Galatians 5:16-24 & 6:8; Romans 8:3-7, 12; Matthew 26:41).

For this reason, taking good care of our bodies through nutrition and exercise is virtually equated with not indulging our bodies with what it desires, but rather doing the exact opposite, for I can not think of a single thing that is healthy to eat that tastes better than everything that is unhealthy to eat. Nor can I think of any healthy activity that brings more immediate pleasure than all of the unhealthy activities that bring immediate pleasure.

1 Thessalonians 5:23 instructs us to be "sanctified entirely" (set apart) in spirit, soul and body; to be "preserved complete without blame" at the coming of our Lord Jesus Christ. That is much more demanding than abstaining from a donut or participating in an occasional game of horseshoes. Jeremiah (12:5) puts the standard physically out of reach, "If you have raced with men on foot and they have tired you out, how can you compete with horses? If you stumble in safe country, how will you manage in the thickets by the Jordan?" Jeremiah's bar is set to the spiritual standard.

The ancient physician, Luke, couples life and existence through movement: "For in him we live and move and have our being" (Acts 17:28 NIV). Luke makes a sandwich, if you will, with life and existence, as the two pieces of bread, but the meat in the middle is physical movement. Two thousand years later, Ratey (2008), associate clinical professor of psychiatry at Harvard Medical School, stated that when we exercise, especially if the exercise requires complex motor movement, we are also exercising the brain areas involved in the full suite of cognitive functions. We are causing the brain to fire signals along the same network of cells, solidifying their connections. Nussbaum (2003) suggested that physical exercise alone might be the critical factor for neural changes within an enriched environment because all measures affected by such environments have not been dissociated from exercise. Robert Sapolsky (2004) concluded that Adult neurogenesis is now the hottest topic in neuroscience. Finally, Paul likens the life of a follower of God to the life of an athlete:

> Do you not know that in a race all the runners run, but only one gets the prize? Run in such a way as to get the prize. Everyone who competes in the games goes into strict training. They do it to get a crown that will not last, but we do it to get a crown that will last forever. Therefore I do not run like someone running aimlessly; I do not fight like a boxer beating the air. No, I strike a blow to my body and make it my slave so that after I have preached to others, I myself will not be disqualified for the prize" (1. Corinthians 9: 24-27, NIV).

Essentially, Paul is saying in life, like a race, merely being alive and living is not enough. One has to live with a goal. Otherwise, one is only shadow boxing. Running to win means hearing the start signal and coming out of the starting blocks with as much force as possible, staying in your line by remaining focused on the goal, and running through the goal line as if it were perpetually 2 meters ahead. Many a winner has lost by failing at one of these three stages; YouTube is full of such sport fails. Thus, to not become disqualified, either in sport or in life, one has to train to the point that one makes their body their slave. For gold medals are eventually forgotten, but the experience of hard work, dedication, and determination reward a lifetime. And if the hard work, dedication, and determination are focused toward the love of God, then the rewards are not limited to this lifetime but carry into the next.

In conclusion, loving God and others through our bodies means giving our bodies only what it needs, while depriving it of what it wants, working hard to become strong, physically, mentally, and emotionally; and, using these strengths to serve others in love through our behaviors and actions.

The Heart: The Symbolic Source of Emotion

The heart that is the organ 'heart' is, of course, also a part of the body, but the term 'heart' is also commonly used to refer to our human emotions. The fact that the term 'heart' is used to refer to the fleshy organ as well as our emotions again illustrates how intricate and these four components are interwoven. To love God and others with all of our hearts means to love with passion. My dictionary defines passion as a strong, almost uncontrollable emotion. Doing something with passion means the motivation to do it goes beyond want and desire and becomes necessary. Artists and athletes often describe the pursuit of their art or sport as a passion in that when asked why they do what they do; they will often answer, "I have to." As such, having a passion for something can be a very fulfilling enterprise, so much so that it becomes a significant part of one's identity. Ask a passionate painter who they are, and they will say, "I am a painter." Ask a passionate football player who they are, and they will say, "I am a football player." Ask a passionate chemist who they are, and they will say, "I am a chemist." Ask a passionate Christian who they are, and they should say, "I am a servant of God." For to love God means to obey his commandments (John 14:15), and His commandment is to be a servant (John 21:15-17), and being a servant of God means being a servant to others (Matthew 25: 35-40); and serving God passionately means that this servanthood is one's greatest treasure (Matthew 6:21; Luke 12:34). We will begin this discussion by examining how and why we become emotional and what happens when we do. This is referred to as the emotional process.

The Emotional Process

Gardiner, Metcalf, and Beebe-Center (1970) outlined the history of the scientific study of emotion, which began with the Greek Philosopher Empedocles in 490 BCE. Empedocles taught that men think and feel pleasure and pain through somatic elements, which were believed to connect the body's emotional feelings to the mind through the bloodstream. As such, the heart was believed to be the center of emotional processing, as it is still often metaphorically believed to be. In 460 BCE, Diogenes added that the feelings of pleasure and pain depend on the circulation of the blood in that good circulation leads to pleasure, while poor circulation leads to pain. At about the same time, Hippocrates was the first to associate consciousness with emotion. He claimed that the four bodily fluids, blood, yellow bile, black bile, and phlegm, were responsible for an individual's temperament. An excess or dearth of one or more of these humors (humor is the Latin word for fluid) determined an individual's temperament. Hippocrates outlined four distinct temperaments: Sanguine (optimistic and social), choleric (short-tempered and irritable), melancholic (reserved and pensive), phlegmatic (relaxed and peaceful) (The Colour Works, 2011). Based on the reddening of the face, which is associated with various emotions, the temperature of the brain was believed to be regulated through the humors. Thus, emotional stability was thought to be maintained through the balance of the four humors (Gardiner et al., 1970).

Hippocrates was the first to record scientific observations pertaining to emotion in terms of the four humors outlined above. Although this was, of course, completely wrong, one may conclude that the significance of the somatic processes of emotion was recognized. Rene Descartes followed suit and also claimed that emotion was a somatic process that did not require mental contribution (Hatfield, 2007). As obscure as this idea may be, we have now learned that much of the emotional process does occur outside of one's conscious awareness (Bucci, 2001, 2002, 2003).

In 1890, William James, who is considered by many as the founder of modern scientific psychology, developed the first modern model of emotion, which still stands as a basis of the understanding we have of emotional processing today. To be fair, Carl Lange developed a very similar theory, independently from James, but at almost the exact same time. The James/Lange theory of emotional processing outlined a four-step process. First, an emotionally provoking stimulus (EPS) is perceived. In the second step, this EPS is evaluated by some means that is still completely unknown today. If the evaluation of the EPS deems an emotional response is suitable, then in the third step of the process, an emotional episode commences and originates in the body in the form of emotional sensations or feelings. According to James, only after emotional feelings are felt in the body does one then, in the fourth step, become aware of the emotion in the mind. Thus, at this point, one may become consciously aware of one's emotional state. Still today, this is a revolutionary idea because it suggests that one does not weep when one is sad, but rather one is sad when one weeps, which seems very counter-intuitive. I think James explains it best and many others do as well, because in many works on the study of emotion quote these words:

> "My theory, on the contrary, is that the bodily changes follow directly the perception or the exciting fact, and that our feeling of the same changes as they occur IS the emotion. ... If we fancy some strong emotion, and then try to abstract from our consciousness of it all the feelings of its bodily symptoms, we find we have nothing left behind, no 'mind stuff' out of which the emotion can be constituted, and that a cold and neutral state of intellectual perception is all that remains.... What kind of an emotion of fear would be left if the feeling neither of quickened heart beats nor of shallow breathing, neither of trembling lips nor of weakened limbs, neither of goose flesh nor of visceral stirrings, were present, it is quite impossible for me to think. Can one fancy the state of rage and picture no ebullition in the chest, no flushing of the face, no dilation of the nostrils, no clenching of the teeth, no impulse to vigorous action, but in their stead limp muscles, calm breathing, and placid face. The present writer, for one, certainly cannot."

However, in 1927 Walter Cannon conducted a series of experiments, which seemingly refuted the James/Lange theory. Cannon agreed with the first two steps of the James/Lange Theory, in that an emotional episode begins with the perception of an EPS, followed by some unknown evaluation of this process. However, Cannon claimed that immediately after the perception and evaluation of an EPS, it is the conscious or subconscious awareness of emotion, cognitively, that then leads to the somatic reactions that we perceive as emotional feelings. Cannon's conclusion is based on a series of experiments. He surgically severed the spinal cord of various animals and presented these animals with EPS, and found that they still reacted emotionally despite having no feelings in their bodies. That is, Cannon claimed that one, of course, weeps when one is sad, and not the other way around.

Since then, empirical evidence has been found, which supports both theories. Thus, the debate between the significance of the body and brain, pertaining to emotional processing, still continues today. Thus, human emotion is still a mystery of science. Ironically, with all the modern technology we have today, we have gained no greater understanding of the second step, the EPS evaluation, than James and Cannon had then. All we know is that this evaluation does indeed take place, but the manner and nature of this evaluation are still more or less completely unknown. In fact, on the subject of emotional processing, modern science has contributed to generating many more questions than answers.

Different stimuli lead different people to an initiation of an emotional stimulus, and we do not know why that is. A vast amount of theories have been conceived, but the data is so confounding and conflicting that we simply do not know much about this evaluation step of the process. In my dissertation, I took a poke at this mystery, and my data ended up pointing in the exact opposite direction of my hypothesis.

What we do know is that after an EPS is perceived, either consciously or even non-consciously, a cognitive evaluation of this EPS takes place. Antonio Damasio's Somatic Marker Hypothesis (2000, 2006) suggested that this evaluation takes place on a binary scale of good and bad. If the evaluation of an EPS yields a positive result, then a positive emotion will ensue, and if the evaluation yields a negative result, then negative emotions will arise. Finally, if an EPS evaluation is deemed neither good nor bad, then no emotional episode will be initiated. Behavioral experiments support this claim; however, the evaluation of an EPS is so incredibly fast; we simply lack the technology to observe and record the exact moment in which an emotional episode is initiated. Through brain imaging technology, we can see when the brain is in an emotional state and when it is not. Therefore, we know there has to be a moment when it momentarily becomes emotional. Nevertheless, the nature of this moment is still a mystery.

Like a muscle, the emotional process either kicks in or does not; there is no such thing as being slightly emotional. An emotion can be weak or strong, but it is either present or not. Our sensory integration processes, in which our senses scan our environment for relevant and essential information, is a continual and constant process. This enables us to be subconsciously attentive to danger and other situations in which we may have to react quickly and in a specific manner. This is supported by studies that have shown that humans can instantly and subconsciously recognize the emotional facial expression of basic emotions (Gosselin et al., 1995; Carrol & Russel, 1996; Dimberg et al., 2000).

Thus, when we are emotional, this means our emotional processing system has perceived an emotionally provocative stimulus (EPS) and has evaluated this EPS and determined that it is significantly good or bad on a purely subjective and binary scale. It is imperative to understand the subjectivity of this process. This means that each individual person evaluates EPS according to their own scale, which is defined through their own life experiences, personality, attitude, character, identity, and everything else that makes each person unique. For this reason, it is actually inherently incorrect when we say, 'this or that makes me happy, sad, afraid, etc. Emotions are not projected from extraneous objects or situations. Our emotional states come out of us and are not projected on to us from our environment. If this were not the case, we would all have significantly similar reactions to the same EPS. The proof of this is simple and found, for example, in the final score in any sporting event. Some people will be happy with the result of the contest, and others will be disappointed.

How the emotional process continues after an EPS has been evaluated and deemed significantly good or bad is widely disputed. Various models of emotional processing have been developed since William James & Carl Lange created the first modern theory of emotional processing. But practically all modern theories of emotional processing are based, to some extent, on the James/Lange and Cannon theories of emotion. Today, it is generally understood that upon the evaluation of an EPS and the consequent initiation of an emotional episode, sensations of the body may lead to the mental perception of the emotion or the cognitive perception of emotion may lead to emotional feelings in the body. In addition to this, Izard (1993) found that emotional states in themselves can lead to the initiation of additional emotional episodes. That is, when we are already feeling one emotion, others are more likely to arise. And, with a greater understanding of the nature of neurotransmitters, it has been found that neurochemical processes may initiate emotional episodes. For example, when one is intoxicated with alcohol, one is more likely to become emotional. Thus, emotions may arise out of the body, in terms of neurochemical processes in the brain as well as emotional somatic processes, aka emotional feelings.

Similarly, emotions may arise out of the mind in terms of preexisting emotional states. This outlines only some of the theories on how we come to be emotional. Paul Ekman's theory of basic emotions addresses the question, what purpose emotions may serve.

The Theory of Basic Emotions

While Psychology has not come to a consensus as to what exactly emotions are or how the process works exactly, the purpose that emotions serve is more widely understood. Most researchers will formulate a similar answer to the question: What purpose do emotions serve?

Most psychologists will agree that each of the basic emotions serves a specific purpose; however, they do not agree on which emotions are basic and what the criterion for a basic emotion is, as opposed to a secondary emotion. Because this discussion would completely explode the boundaries of this book, I will offer here only a very simplified definition based on the findings of Paul Ekman. Ekman found that humans worldwide, regardless of society or civilization, all shared a finite number of basic facial expressions, which were found to be universally and reliably mapped to specific emotions. These emotions were then deemed basic emotions. The six basic emotions found nearly on every list of basic emotions are joy, sadness, anger, fear, disgust, and surprise.

In the most basic sense, emotions are a catalyst for behavior. As such, each specific emotion fosters the initiation of a specific behavior. This is because humans are programmed to avoid false negatives. A false negative is an error in perception, which improperly indicates no presence of danger when real danger is indeed present.

A false negative can be a fatal mistake. Humans are programmed to avoid false-negative mistakes. Assuming no danger where, in fact, the danger is, does not lead to a long life. Therefore, humans and most other animals are rather safe than sorry. Examples of false negatives would be the assumption that something is ok to eat when it is not or the assumption that the rustling in the bush is not a tiger when it is a tiger. Such a false negative can lead to death, while a false positive, thinking something is bad to eat when it is not, leads only to hunger rather than immediate death.

For this reason, we have the emotion of disgust, which prompts us to turn away from potentially harmful elements. Similarly, being afraid of something that is not dangerous is not nearly as bad as not being afraid of something dangerous. As such, each of these basic emotions can be defined in terms of how they influence our behavior.

Each of the basic emotions tells us something about ourselves or our environment without us having to think about it with the comparatively slow process of conscious awareness. Thus, emotions assert in us an impulse to behave in a certain way towards emotionally provocative stimuli. For example, the emotion of joy tells us instinctively what we like. This emotion gives us the impulse to laugh and smile. This, in turn, releases endorphins that make us feel good. The pleasure principle asserts that when we experience joy, we want more of that which we associate with that experience. Thus, if I meet someone or do something and smile and experience joy, I will be prompted to meet this person or do this activity more often in the near future.

The emotion of sadness instinctively tells us that we have to cope with a significant loss. If I lose my keys and cannot find them, then I do not get sad. Instead, I continue to look for them. If I lose my cat, I will also initially look for it, but if I do not find it within a reasonable amount of time, sadness will set in, and I will come to the realization that it is gone, and I will stop looking for it. This is an extremely delicate process, for imagine what would happen if we got sad when we lost our keys. We would sit and cry and not look for them, and eventually conclude that we have to find another means of transportation. Or what would happen if we did not get sad when we lost our cat, we would continue looking for it for the rest of our lives and most likely neglect other important things in the process. Thus, if someone very dear to me dies, then my emotion of sadness will prompt me to do something that will help me come to terms with the loss so that I can continue with my life.

The emotion of anger instinctively tells me what is important to me. When we get angry about something, then this emotion prompts behavior to do something about it. If someone insults me and I get angry, then that tells me that this person's opinion is important to me, or my honor is important to me, or something about this situation or the people involved is important to me. If someone breaks a rule, which makes me angry, this tells me that this rule is important to me. Hence, if someone seems to get angry very fast and easy, it is probably because too many things are important to this person.

On the other hand, if someone hardly ever gets angry about anything, then it may be because they do not care significantly about much.

Thus, when we get angry about something, then we are prompted to do something about the object of our anger. To react TO our anger, as opposed to IN our anger, means that as issues come up, and we feel the emotion of anger arise in our body before we allow the emotion to override our cognitive processes, we react to the emotion and reflect upon it.

When one reacts in anger, one allows the emotional processes to switch from cognitive thought to survival thought modus. When that happens, people often do and say things they later regret. However, when we become consciously aware of this anger. Then we think about the situation, identify why it makes us angry, determine what can be done about it, and then do it. To react in anger means to experience a situation in which something important to me in some way is violated, and then to attack this violation without first becoming consciously aware of what precisely this violation is. While this may be an effective means of resolving anger, if the object of the anger is someone of relational significance, they are likely to respond with anger, causing more anger until everyone is angry, and no one knows why they are angry.

For this reason, it is always better to react to one's anger than to react in one's anger. In addition to this, it is perhaps equally bad to suppress anger. For if something or someone that is significantly important to you is violated in some way and anger arises in you, and you suppress this anger, eventually the proverbial straw that broke the camel's back will lead to an anger explosion that to everyone else will seem like an unjustified amplified reaction, which is very likely to lead to more anger. Ephesians 4: 26 sums this up very well: "In your anger do not sin: Do not let the sun go down while you are still angry." This does not mean it is wrong to be angry. Instead, it is a warning that one should take care to react TO one's anger, but not IN one's anger, which also implies that one should take care not to suppress one's anger.

The emotion of fear instinctively tells us what not to do. One may say that the emotion of fear keeps one from doing stupid things. If I am climbing up in a very high tree, at some point, fear will prompt me not to climb any higher. If I am not a very experienced climber, this may happen as soon as I get much higher than the point, from which a fall may lead to significant bodily harm. If I am an experienced climber, this may not happen until the thinner branches at the top of the tree begin to crack under my weight. To keep climbing after that point would simply be stupid. Similarly, driving a car at optimal conditions, one may not experience fear, depending on one's driving ability and experience, until one reaches 100 miles per hour. But the same speed in the dark, on windy roads, and while it is snowing should induce fear, prompting one to slow down.

In some psychological conditions, one may experience too much fear or too little. When one has too little fear, then one can greatly overestimate one's self and cause harm to themselves or others. When one has too much fear in situations where no significant danger is apparent, one may neglect to act in situations in which action is utterly important. This is commonly referred to as anxiety, a topic that will be discussed in greater detail momentarily. However, for now, Philippians 4:6-7 addresses the topic of anxiety as well needed:

"Do not be anxious about anything, but in every situation, by prayer and petition, with thanksgiving, present your requests to God. And the peace of God, which transcends all understanding, will guard your hearts and your minds in Christ Jesus" (NIV).

The emotion of disgust instinctively tells us what might be harmful to our health. This may be primarily associated with food and drink; however, the feeling of disgust may also be experienced in other areas of our life. Disgust may be experienced in association with relationships, habits, activities, and essentially anything that has the potential to cause us harm. The emotion of disgust prompts us to avoid the object of our disgust. In fact, the feeling of disgust is so repelling it literally turns our nose away.

Each of these basic emotions corresponds to a particular muscle in the face, which has the sole purpose of projecting the corresponding emotion. The wrinkling of the nose is the tale-tell sign of disgust. Fear is expressed by the widening of the mouth. Anger is expressed through the pulling together of the eyebrows, while sadness is projected by raising the inner eyebrows while excluding the outer eyebrows. It is very difficult to isolate the inside of the eyebrow from the outside of the eyebrow. The muscle responsible for this is called the AU 1. The difficulty we have in isolating this muscle is that it is primarily driven by the automatic nervous system rather than the central nervous system. That means our face projects emotions without us having to think about doing so. Of course, we do have access to some of our facial muscles, but not necessarily all of them equally. With practice, one can obtain the ability to isolate the AU1 muscle, but the key to it is method acting. Think of something sad, and you will start to feel the AU1 twitch, and you may even feel a little sadness in your body due to your greater awareness through the attempt to isolate the muscle.

So while we have complete access to the muscle of your mouth, we can try to fake a smile. But if we are not genuinely happy, our cheeks will not rise (AU6). Such a smile will seem fake. While conducting my dissertation study, I set up a science fair-like booth with various attractions about facial expression. In one of the attractions, 12 various smiles were displayed, and I asked people if they could guess which smile was the genuine smile identifiable by the expression of joy (AU 6 + 12). Nearly every person could identify this smile on the first try.

Another action unit that is difficult to isolate actively is the AU 5. This action unite lifts the upper eyelid so that the whites of the eye can be seen above the iris. Think Eddie Murphy as Alex Fowley in Beverly Hills Cop, and you will know his iconic expression of surprise. The emotion of surprise instinctively tells us what is new, unexpected, and significant information. When something surprises us, this prompts us to reevaluate and rethink a situation while integrating the new information with the old. Surprise tells us, 'this changes everything.' When we are surprised, we instinctively begin to reprocess what we have just experienced in order to gain a better understanding of the situation. For example, when one is surprised by the experience of a magician's trick, we know that the lady cannot really be sawed in half and still be acting the way she is. So we instinctively reevaluate what we just saw, knowing that there must be information we had not previously perceived. When we are surprised by the news that we will become a father, then, of course, we know how this happened. Still, we instantly think back and try to remember when this happened and what changes will come to pass due to the new situation. The emotion of surprise prompts our minds to reboot, not unlike a computer update. Incidentally, some include the emotion of disappointment into the list of basic emotions. In contrast, others argue disappointment is merely a combination of sadness and surprise and, therefore, not a basic emotion.

Now that we have identified and defined the basic emotions, I would like to reiterate a previous point. One must do away with a falsehood that is often associated with our perception of these emotions and emotions in general. Have you ever said or heard anyone say, "You make me (insert emotion)." This is an inherently false statement and an unhealthy way of thinking about and reacting to one's emotions. No one and nothing can make anyone feel anything. The feeling and the emotion come from within the person experiencing the emotion and not from the object of the emotion. That is, spiders and snakes do not make anyone afraid. They have no mystic power to cause people to feel afraid or experience the emotion of fear. The proof of this is quite elementary. Imagine six people you specifically know, including yourself, at a breakfast table. And now picture a spider descending from the ceiling directly into the middle of the table. Now ask yourself, would the six people at the table react in the same way? Certainly not. Some may indeed react in fear, but others in disgust or surprise or have no emotional reaction at all. Some may simply kill the spider on sight, while another may want to rescue it and take it outside. The possible reactions are unlimited and also vary in degrees of intensity. If the spider had any power of its own to elicit specific emotional reactions in people, then all people would react much more similar to them.

Thus when we say, this or that or whoever makes me happy, sad, angry, or wherever other emotion one would like to insert here, we are making a drastic mistake. We are deferring the responsibility of our emotions to someone or something else rather than to ourselves. No one else but us is responsible for our emotions. Victor Frankl (1959) put it this way, "Forces beyond your control can take away everything you possess except one thing, your freedom to choose how you will respond to the situation."

While emotions are inherently good, effective, and productive in that they prompt us to specific actions, we as humans are by no means incapable of reacting to them rather than in them. This is what separates humans from animals. While we have drives, instincts, and reflexes, just as the animals do, humans alone, being created in God's image, have the ability to override these impulses. That is, when we are emotional, we are still capable of logical and rational thought, although to do this often requires a conscious effort to do so. Thus, before we strike out in anger and become violent, we can become consciously aware of our anger and say with rational thought, "something has to be done about this," rather than merely becoming aggressive and behaving emotionally. If the emotion is continually suppressed and one neglects to react to the emotion and not even in the emotion, this can lead to a build-up that may lead to an untimely emotional explosion. And when emotions erupt, behaviors become extremely difficult to control, as the emotional processes override conscious and rational thought. Next, we take a closer look at two emotions, fear and sadness, which can lead to the psychological conditions of anxiety and depression, respectively, if one fails to react to the emotions of fear and sadness for a significant amount of time.

Fear and Anxiety

What exactly is anxiety? Well, let us start by defining fear. Fear is the feeling or sense of danger imposed by something, be it a person, place, time, object (real or abstract). The term fear implies that there is some object causing that fear. Thus, the term fear is often followed by the preposition 'of.' One is afraid of this or that or has a fear of this or that. Anxiety, then, is essentially the same feeling, but without the object of the fear. So, if you want to have an idea of what anxiety is like, imagine something you are afraid of. Then imagine that you get that same exact feeling, the same fear, but without the object of that fear, for no apparent reason.

Of all the basic emotions, fear is probably the most prevalent in most people's lives. Yoda may have put it best when he told young Aniken Skywalker, "Fear leads to anger, anger leads to hate, and hate leads to the dark side." Like all emotions, fear does have a practical and productive purpose. It keeps us from doing stupid stuff, as I explained earlier. But much too often, fear becomes too abundant, and it paralyzes us from doing what we want and need to do.

The reason for this, as discussed earlier, is due to the fact that humans are programmed to avoid false negatives. It is ultimately better to be afraid of something that is not truly dangerous than it is not to be afraid of something dangerous. Thus, humans are born with the capability to experience fear. Studies have suggested that the brain scans our environment for things to be afraid of, and it is very efficient and productive in doing so. In one such experiment, individuals were shown a series of pictures, which consisted of nine faces, one of which displayed a threatening face. And although individuals were only shown each picture for a split second, individuals were able to pick out the threatening face (Öhman et al., 2001).

We are born with the ability to recognize fear; however, we are not born with the knowledge of what to fear; that has to be learned. And this begins even before the baby is born. While still in the womb, the baby learns to recognize the mother's voice. In addition to this, the mother's heartbeat has been found to have an effect on the baby (Sieratzki & Woll, 1996). As such, the baby is receptive to the emotional states of the mother even before birth. After birth, emotional facial expression begins to play a significant role in the child's emotional development. If the mother is fearful and nervous, then the baby, innately programmed to recognize facial expressions (Kochanska et al., 2007), will adopt the mother's emotional state. As such, the trait anxiety of the baby will narrow in on the trait anxiety of the mother. During development, the child learns to associate the state of anxiety of the mother with situations in the environment.

If the mom shrieks in the presence of a barking dog, the child will also. If the mother exhibits fear of a spider crawling on the floor, the child will also. The child is born with the capacity to fear but learns through its environment what to fear. The more things a child learns to be afraid of, the more often the child will be in a state of fear. And the more often a child is in a state of fear, the higher the child's trait anxiety will become. This does not mean that such a child will ultimately develop an anxiety disorder as an adult—however, adults who have developed anxiety more often than not associate their childhood experiences with their anxiety. But, not all who have had difficult childhood experiences develop anxiety in their adult years. It is like if it rains, the streets get wet, but if the streets are wet, it does not necessarily mean it rained. Whether or not stress leads to anxiety depends solely upon the individual. Sure, one could argue that one's DNA contributes significantly to the occasion, but as I stated earlier, there is nothing we can do about that now. That is not a problem to solve, but rather a fact to accept.

Through adaptive behavior, we navigate through life, acquiring mannerisms to avoid fear and anxiety. If one is afraid of dogs, then one can simply avoid them. If one is afraid of public speaking, one finds a job in which it is not required. If one does not like social events, one simply develops an interest that one can partake alone. However, problems can arise when coping behavior increases so much that it is no longer coping behavior but rather a restricting behavior. When it gets to the point when one no longer does not merely care much for dogs but rather simply can not function in the presents of a dog. When fear paralyzes the body and the mind so much that neither rational thought nor bodily control is possible, then the issue must be addressed.

Rational Emotional Behavior Therapy (REBT) is one possible method, and it is easily explained. REBT works on the assumption that an individual's core belief of an object of fear is responsible for the triggering of emotion upon the perception of the object. That is, the individual believes something specific about the object, which causes the individual to be afraid of the object (Lazarus, 1982). Thus, in order to remove the fear, one needs only to examine one's core belief.

The REBT asserts that one (A) perceives an Antecedent situation, then (B) associates this with a core Belief, and then (C) Consequent reaction follows. Thus, to identify a core belief, one can first identify the (A): the Antecedent situation and the following (C); consequential reaction. When (A) then (C). When I see a dog, I totally flip out. When this (A), then that (C). The REBT theory asserts that between the (A) and the (C) is a core belief that connects the two. If one can identify this connection, one can test the core belief outside of the realm of emotion. In the above example, one may conclude that their (B) is that the dog is going to kill them. When the (B) is addressed, one can discuss it logically and test the validity of the belief. Through this process, one may come to the conclusion that given any 'normal' situational encounter with a random dog, one could perhaps get snapped or barked at. Still, it is unlikely that the dog is an immediate life threat. Thus, being afraid of a dog bite is healthy respect, but thinking you are going to get eaten up on the spot, is a core belief that, when challenged, could be nullified. This would then change the individual's (C) in association with (A) due to a new (B). This same process can be used with anxiety disorders, but the process is more abstract because there is no object of fear in the case of anxiety, only the feeling of fear. When an individual is suddenly overcome by the feeling of fear, although there is no perceived presence of an object of that fear, then this is what is referred to as a panic attack.

If the mere thought of a dog induces fear, one can distract one's mind and thus significantly reduce or eliminate the immediate fear. But if one simply out of the blue is overcome with the intense feeling of immediate danger, but without a conscious awareness of what the object of that danger could be, neither through one's physical senses nor in one's imagination (mind), then what can one do? The body begins to react as if it is being attacked, but there is no attacker. This can lead to a panic attack. People who suffer from this often think they are having a heart attack, which induces more fear and worsens the problem, causing them to think that their death is immediate, causing more fear, and the problem gets worse and worse, which could possibly induce a true heart attack.

Discovering one's core belief in association with panic attacks is a long and weary process. But at the basis of this core belief will be the basic fear of death. Thus, from a theological perspective, if one could remove the core fear of death, one could eliminate panic attacks. If one established the teachings from the Bible as core beliefs in their everyday lives, then one can essentially live fearlessly. I say essentially because fear, in the sense of respect, is what keeps us from doing stupid things. For "the fear of the Lord is the beginning of wisdom, and knowledge of the Holy One is understanding" (Proverbs 9:10).

Psalm 119: 11, and Hebrews 8:10 tells us to store up the word of God in our hearts and minds. What happens when we memorize scripture from a psychological perspective. The walls of my office are plastered with A6 size notes of various Bible verses. I do not have them all memorized verbatim, but I know them pretty well. Probably about half of them have to do with some aspect of fear and anxiety. I am susceptible to life stress like any other person, but when feelings of anxiety arise in me, I am, first of all, in tune with my body. The feeling of anxiety is often felt first in the body before one is consciously aware of the emotion of fear. Thus a good way to combat anxiety is to locate the part of your body from which the feeling of fear or stress arises. For me, it is in the jaw muscles. I mentally check in with my jaw muscles regularly. If I find that they are tense, I ask myself if I am worried about anything. And when I do that, I often suddenly become aware that I had been preoccupied with a particular problem.

It takes a while until one can locate a source of stress in a particular body part because it requires rational thought to discern from which body part the feelings of anxiety originate when the panic attack itself makes rational thinking difficult. Nevertheless, discerning where in the body the feelings are coming from may help limit the intensity and duration of the panic attack.

Sometimes it seems as though negative thoughts just appear out of nowhere in our minds, leading to a panic attack. However, some psychologists would agree with James (1890) if the negative emotions exist in your mind, they were already in your body, but you just didn't become consciously aware of it until the bad thought hit your mind. This is where I have found scripture memory to be extremely helpful. When one memorizes Philippians 4:6, "Do not be anxious about anything, but in every situation, by prayer and petition with thanksgiving, present your requests to God. And the peace of God, which transcends all understanding will guard your hearts and your minds," then, when worrying thoughts come into my mind, thoughts of this verse are triggered as well. My core belief is that all things work together for good for those who love God and are called according to his name (Romans 8:28), and the anxiety is significantly reduced.

So, when fear or even stress arises in me, it causes me to check if I am walking with God or not. If I am not, I probably have every reason to be afraid, and I better take care of something in my life. But if the sense of fear arises, and I check and see that I am walking with God, then I am able to shake off the feeling of fear and fearful thoughts relatively quickly.

As previously stated, to figure out what can be done about a disorder, one has to break it down from the perspective of the heart, body, mind, and soul. So, in the case of anxiety disorder, the mind and soul offer little insight at first. The person does not know of any thoughts, conscious or subconscious, that seem to be related to the emotional feeling of fear. (If this were the case, then we would be discussing a phobia, rather than anxiety). Thus, we see that in the case of anxiety, it is the heart (emotions) that is wreaking havoc on the body. Indeed, psychology has shown that it is through the body that we become consciously aware of our emotional state. As William James pointed out in 1890 that if it were not for the sensation of accelerated heartbeat, cold sweat, shallow breath, we would not know that we were afraid.

Thus, when working with people with anxiety, ask them where in their body, do they first begin to feel the feeling of fear in them swelling. A question, which, when first heard for the first time, sets them back for a moment, leaving them pondering, but after a moment, brings forth significant insight. Most of them have never thought about that, but all of them, with relatively little effort, are able to give a clear and concise answer.

For some, it is in the jaw, others the stomach, hands, neck, knees... Essentially everyone I have ever worked with on this matter was able to express where in their body the anxiety is first felt. Encouraging, as it may seem, that is the easy part. Now, having pinpointed the telltale body part, the first domino of a long series of dominos, the difficult part is maintaining a conscious awareness of this body part, like a bobber in the water while fishing. When the telltale sensation begins, the difficult thing to do is to extract this domino from the row to deter the chain reaction. This is not easy and requires some practice, but in doing so, an interesting thing will happen, as one gets better and better at catching this first domino before it sets off the others.

Sadness and Depression

As I mentioned earlier, the emotion of sadness instinctively tells us that we have to cope with a significant loss. Recall the example of my lost keys: If I lose my keys and cannot find them, I do not get sad. Instead, I continue to look for them. If I lose my cat, I will also initially look for it, but if I do not find it within a reasonable amount of time, sadness will set in, and I will come to the realization that it is gone, and I will stop looking for it. This is an extremely delicate process, for imagine what would happen if we got sad when we lost our keys. We would sit and cry and not look for them, and eventually come to the conclusion that we have to find another means of transportation. Or what would happen if we did not get sad when we lost our cat, we would continue looking for it for the rest of our lives and most likely neglect other important things in the process. Thus, if someone very dear to me dies, then my emotion of sadness will prompt me to do something that will help me come to terms with the loss to continue with my life.

As I mentioned before, God created us with emotions, and these emotions have a good and productive purpose. The emotion of sadness has the function of letting us know what we have lost. This, combined with daily life stress, can lead to a big problem if one is sad about having lost things that are not important anyway. But, if we read God's word and have inscribed in our hearts and minds, then we become less concerned with things that will not last and concentrate on eternal things. If you do this, then depression will never be a problem.

REBT can also be used to treat depression. Similar to what we have discussed about anxiety, clinical depression may result from a negative core belief. To do this, one tries to become aware of the activating event and the resulting consequence. For example, when I see happy couples, sadness overcomes me, and I feel lonely and cry. Between this A and C lies a negative core belief that must be defined and then challenged. For example, if a person believes in the core of their being that they are unlovable, then the person will have to challenge that core belief then and find out if they are indeed unlovable. Perhaps this person has no friends, no family, and works alone. As such, they are hardly ever at social events where they may have the opportunity to make a good connection with someone so that a quality relationship might take root. Instead, they may only meet people when they and everybody else are out and about, busy with everyday life and work. Such a lifestyle could indeed lead someone to believe they are unlovable because every time they meet someone, it is only on the go while people have their minds set on accomplishing daily tasks. If situational occurrences such as mobbing and other forms of abuse have also been experienced, this would significantly strengthen a negative core belief.

Therefore hope is of the utmost importance. When one has developed a negative core belief, one must challenge it and conclude that the negative core belief is not true. To do this, one has to have a significant amount of hope that it is not true to withstand the vigorous stress that arises when trying to change their core beliefs.

Memorizing Bible verses are again a beneficial therapy from both the theological and psychological perspectives. From a psychological perspective, positive affirmation has been found to have a significant positive effect on one's emotional state (Rogers, 1951; Norcross, 2002). From a theological perspective, if one has the core belief that "...God so loved the world that he gave his one and only Son, that whoever believes in him shall not perish but have eternal life" (John 3:16), then will experience sadness in life, but they will not suffer from it.

Emotional Communication

The topic of emotional communication illustrates the intricacy between the heart and the mind, for emotional communication could be described as straddling the fence between them. Willamina Bucci (1995, 2001, 2002, 2003) outlined three levels of communication with respect to the degree of conscious awareness in which they are processed. The verbal-symbolic level of communication is simply speech, which takes place within the realm of conscious awareness. Verbal-symbolic means that communication is taking place in the form of sounds and that these sounds represent standardized meanings. For example, if while you are reading these words, you look up to someone and say "tree," the person may be very perplexed in why you have done this, but they will nevertheless instantly understand the meaning of the sound, which is represented by the letters, t r e e. This level of communication operates at the highest level of conscious awareness. While one may not always be consciously aware of what one is saying, one is usually consciously aware that one is speaking. Unless, of course, one is talking in one's sleep or is suffering from a neurological disorder such as Tourette.

The next highest level of communication is non-verbal symbolic communication. This means that communication is taking place in the form of actions and that these actions have symbolic meaning. This is essentially sign language. Some examples of such communication would be the nodding of the head in yes and no directions, the shrugging of the shoulders, the thumbs up, the middle finger up, the rolling of the eyes, and many other actions that have defined symbolic meaning. This form of communication may take place inside one's conscious awareness; however, it may also occur without being consciously aware that it is taking place. Sometimes people are clearly aware that they are shaking their head "no," rolling their eyes, or demonstrating some other form of non-verbal symbolic communication, but sometimes they are not.

The non-verbal non-symbolic level of communication is more commonly known as body language. However, because the term language directly implies symbolism, the term body language is misleading and inherently incorrect. Such communications take place in the form of actions, which, in and of themselves, have no symbolic meaning. Nevertheless, such unspoken and unintended communication has been found to significantly contribute to communication as a whole. Bucci pointed out that a much more accurate term for this level of communication is emotional communication because it is essentially exactly that: a projection of our emotion from moment to moment. While this level of communication generally takes place completely outside of one's conscious awareness, through practice and training, one is able to increase one's level of conscious awareness of their emotional communication. This is what actors are trained to do.

With his iceberg diagram, Walter Bartussek (2000) illustrated very well how these three levels of communication work together. Imagine, if you will, an Iceberg floating in the water. It is common knowledge that a much greater percentage of the iceberg's volume is underwater, while only a small part of it is above the water. Suppose we allow the water level to represent the boundary between conscious awareness and non-conscious unawareness and understand that this boundary is continually in motion as the iceberg bobs in the waves. In that case, we have a fairly accurate description of the human mind. One's level of conscious awareness is not a fixed state of mind. For example, you have most likely been completely unaware of the feeling of the chair you are sitting on until now. But now, having read these words, your mind is collecting data pertaining to the sensation of your butt. Now you are consciously aware of the hardness of the chair; if it squeaks, its stability. You could probably even give an accurate assessment of the temperature. Furthermore, this raised consciousness is likely to have caused you to adjust your body in the chair so that now you are sitting more comfortably than before.

So, forget about your chair now and focus again on the iceberg. If two icebergs are floating near each other, the distance between the icebergs' top tips will be greater than the distance between their bases underwater. Now, when we correspond this to two people who are communicating, the distance between them is the same regardless of the level of communication; however, the time it takes for the communication to take place differs significantly. Speech is a very slow and complex process. Before a thought can be formulated and spoken, it must pass through five distinct areas of the brain with different specific functions before the thought comes out of the mouth in the form of speech. So, imagine you were traveling from A to B, and you have to change trains, planes, or automobiles five times. The chances that you may arrive late increase with the number of connections you have to take.

Figure 2 Bartussek's (2000) Ice Berg Model of Communication

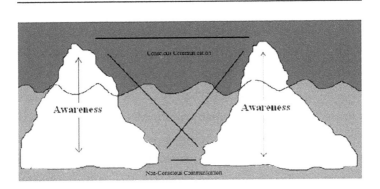

From Bewusst sein im Körper [Consciousness in Body] (p.16), by Walter Bartussek, 2000, Mainz, Germany, Matthias Grünwald Verlag,. Copyright 2000 by Walter Bartussek, Adapted with permission.

Emotional communication, on the other hand, is incredibly fast. It is often compared with or described as a reflex. While the central nervous system controls verbal communication, emotional communication is significantly controlled by the autonomic nervous system, which is rooted in the brain stem and controls such functions as heartbeat, breathing, and reflexes. Emotional communication takes place so fast that one is seldom aware that it is taking place at all. However, with very close friends, one may, at times, be seemingly in sync and able to communicate without words, in a "are you thinking what I am thinking?" kind of manner. This is also the communication level between improvisation actors, team sports, and other such groups where people seem to know what the other person is doing and thinking without having to communicate it verbally.

The diagonal lines of communication, as illustrated above, represents communication which is projected consciously- but perceived unconsciously, or communication projected unconsciously but perceived consciously. This is often referred to as incongruent sensitivity (De Gelder, 2006). For example, imagine a man coming home who verbally communicates, "Hi, honey. I'm home. Is dinner ready?" as he consciously looks about to see if there is something for him to do to help. However, the wife may perceive his action unconsciously and therefore increasing the chance of misinterpreting his actions incorrectly. For example, she may interpret his behavior as a sign of impatience and may respond verbally according to her perceptions.

Or similarly, the man, being unconscious of his nonverbal communication, looking about for whatever reason, could inadvertently send a message, which the woman consciously but also incorrectly perceives. She might perceive this action as an attempt to dominate and take over the cooking and again may respond verbally according to her perceptions. This corresponds directly with Bucci's (2001) argument that interactions that may appear super sensory or supernatural may be accounted for through observable sensory means. Cues that are projected, intentionally and unintentionally, by one individual and perceived, intentionally and unintentionally, by another may or may not be expressed verbally in return; nevertheless, a communication transfer may still take place. While such incongruities cannot completely be eliminated, one might suggest that through increasing one's awareness of emotional communication, the degree and frequency of such incongruities could be reduced. In any case, one could argue that many disputes have their origin in this sort of diagonal communication.

In addition to this, if one has obtained a greater awareness of emotional communication, one can use the diagonal communication lines to increase the productivity in their communication. While communicating verbally, one can also be consciously aware of the emotional communication one is sending with their verbal communication. One can not only perceive another person's verbal communication within the realm of conscious awareness but also remain consciously aware of a person's emotional communications, which inadvertently accompany their verbal communications, giving one greater insight as to what the person is communicating.

Now that we have addressed how humans communicate with each other, let us examine for a moment how God communicates with us. Since we are made in God's image, one might expect to find that there may be some similarities in the nature of His communication with us with respect to how we communicate with each other. God also communicates with us on three different levels, through the Bible. The Bible is often referred to as the inspired Word of God. However, that is often challenged by many who claim that it was only mortal and imperfect men who wrote these words so long ago. To this, a devoted Christian may claim that these men were inspired to write what they did. This line of discussion will then inevitably lead to an unproductive and endless debate because of historical matters such as, who wrote what, when, and why cannot be resolved scientifically. The fact of the matter is that the 'inspiration' in God's inspired Word is/was and never will be in the writing of the Holy Scriptures, but rather the inspiration of and from God comes only through the reading of the Holy Scriptures. The proof of this is simple. Assume we had a document here in our possession for everybody to see; and, it was absolutely, without a doubt, known to have come directly from the hand of God. It would still do nobody any good whatsoever until it was read. Therefore, in the inspired Word of God, the inspiration lies only in the reading of it, not in the writing of it. Reading the Bible corresponded to the verbal level of communicating as described previously by Bucci, but God communicates with us not only on this level.

Like the three levels of communication that scientific psychology has discovered, God can communicate with us on three similar levels. First, corresponding to the first level of simple verbal language, we can read the Bible's words and understand their meaning, especially if we take the time to dig into the original Hebrew and Greek. On this level of communication, we simply take in information, in the same way, one would while reading anything else. We read words and understand the meaning. If one were to remain on this level only, then I believe one would miss out on a significant amount of what God wants to communicate to us.

On a deeper level, we can read the emotion. When we ask ourselves what went on in Abraham's mind and heart when God asked him to sacrifice his son, Joseph, when he was sold into slavery and wrongly imprisoned, Peter, when he denied Jesus three times, after swearing he would never do that. Or, one could pose the same question of characters in moments of positive affect. What did David think and feel as he watched Goliath fall? Have you ever imagined what it would feel like to walk through the Red Sea as God parts the waters? The Bible is not only meant to be read in the brain but also in the heart and soul as well. And when one does this, one may find that all of the emotional situations told through the words of the Bible are situations that we have also experienced and felt. I have never killed a giant or walked through parted waters, but I wake up every day with a broken body and still manage to carry on. I have never denied knowing Jesus, direct to his face, but I have denied people help, which, according to Matthew 25:40, is the same thing.

When one reads the Bible for emotional content, then one finds that the words do not only express meaning but also emotion. One may suggest that the mark of a good book is its emotional content. However, in that case, the Bible is not only a good book; it is much more. Not only can one contemplate the heart and mind of the characters in the Bible, but one also finds situations in the Bible that correspond to the situations and experiences we all have today. In fact, I have never come across a situation or an experience in my life or the life of someone else that could not be related to a passage or story in the Bible. Any situation or event, as horrible as one can imagine, or as great as one could imagine, can be found in the Bible.

Finally, sometimes God just speaks directly to our souls. Sometimes I will read a passage that I have read 100 times or more before. And then, suddenly, I will understand an entirely new meaning behind the very same passage. Just a moment ago, I watched a sermon on the internet because we are all here in the Corona Virus quarantine. The Pastor talked about the passage where Jesus prayed in the Garden of Gethsemane, "Abba, Father, everything is possible for you. Take this cup from me. Yet not what I will, but what you will" (Mark 14:36, NIV). The message that is often projected with this passage is a message of submission and trust, a thoroughly equitable message at this coronavirus time. And this is the message that I had always associated with this passage until I began struggling with prayer, healing, and disease. Then one day, this message told me something entirely different: Not even Jesus got all of his prayers answered.

Most of you will not understand this unless you are disabled. But disabled Christians catch a lot of flack from people who question our faith, based on the fact that we have not yet been healed. I have had complete strangers approach me, quoting Isaiah 53:5, "... by his wounds we are healed." So many people have told me that I am still sick only because I lack faith. So, I reflected upon myself and turned to scripture and prayed and meditated, searching for the missing truth, what was I doing wrong. Was my faith really lacking, was there sin in my life that I was not addressing properly? What was I doing wrong? While I was dealing with all of this, I came across the Mark passage, and suddenly I realized: Not even Jesus got all of His Prayers answered, the way he wanted.

After having read that verse so many times before, God used it in a completely different way, to tell me directly in my soul that we are Ok with each other. I do not need to doubt my faithfulness towards Him. Right then and there, I knew I am on track. I am right there where he wants me to be. And that is in this damn wheelchair. But believe me when I tell you, I would rather be in this weak and broken body with God than in the strongest body without Him.

Impulses out of the heart come in the form of emotional episodes, in which the evaluation of the EPS was highly significant, as previously described. As such, the emotional spark that starts an emotional episode is the proverbial emotional flame that is the focus of many songs. However, emotional impulses do not only occur as the spark of an emotional impulse. They often occur when we are already emotional or are in an emotional state. As such, emotions can swell to a point where an impulse from the heart can erupt like a volcano.

Thus, impulses out of the heart are often behaviors that are driven by one's current emotional state. If one is in a somber mood, this will lead to somber behaviors; and, if one is in a joyous mood, this will lead to joyous behaviors. As it is with emotions and has been previously mentioned, usually one is not consciously aware of their emotional state, from which these behavioral impulses come. But others certainly are. For most people, it is not too difficult to determine someone's mood based on their behavior. However, when one becomes consciously aware of their own and the emotional communication of others, this is a skill that one can fine-tune above that which individuals are born.

The Human Mind

As previously stated, to love God and others with all of our minds means to be fully and completely concentrated on His love. To do this requires discipline to remain motivated to do so. That means we have to read the Bible and do this regularly and daily, just as we eat regularly and daily, for man does not live by bread alone (Luke 4:4; Matthew 4:4). For if we do not take in God's Word with the utmost concentration when the time comes to put his Word into practice, one maybe. "...like someone who looks at his face in a mirror and, after looking at himself, goes away and immediately forgets what he looks like. But whoever looks intently into the perfect law that gives freedom, and continues in it – not forgetting what they have heard, but doing it- they will be blessed in what they do" (James 1: 23-25).

Probably the most common source of impulse comes from the mind. Impulses out of mind are perceived as ideas. Generally, most intelligent people think before they do. Ideas generally precede actions. For example, just now, I thought that I had to pick up my daughter in an hour, but I want to finish writing this section first, so I had the impulse to think of an example of an impulse out of the mind quickly. Impulses out of mind make for a controlled but relatively slow action. Collectively, ideas make up what is known as a core belief. Neenan and Dryer (2004) defined core beliefs as underlying assumptions and rules that set standards, which guide one's behavior. Core beliefs are the thoughts and ideas a person has about themselves, which comprise their cognitive identity, in both positive and negative terms. When a person states, "I am who I am," they are referring to their core belief.

These generalized and unconditional ideas are formed through early learning experiences. Our core beliefs consist of things about ourselves that we extremely strongly believe to be true, regardless of whether or not they are indeed true. Our core believes essentially define who we think we are and who we think we are not. As such, core beliefs are very firm structures that are very difficult to change, even if we do come to realize that they are not true. It is relatively elementary that the mind should significantly influence the heart, body, and soul. For example, say a person thinks that they are unattractive, and this becomes a core belief. This core belief may cause a susceptibility to sadness or other negative emotions, which then, in turn, will affect the body in terms of status. Thus, this person may develop bad posture, which in turn reinforces the core belief. Similarly, having the core belief of unattractiveness may suppress impulses to dress up and groom oneself, which again will only reinforce the core belief.

The mind, unlike the brain, is not made up of living cell tissue. In fact, one could, and some have argued that the mind does not really exist. It has been suggested that the mind, whatever it is, is contained in the brain and can be reduced to the brain's neuro-processes. The human mind is difficult to grasp; however, William James (1890) 'Mind Stuff' theory does a good job of pointing out with a series of examples how intangible the human mind is with respect to the human brain. We know, without a doubt, that thought occurs in the brain. But how is it that someone could lose their mind but still have their brain? The mind and the brain are intricately related but separate none the less. As previously stated, the mind is essentially the abstract and intangible iCloud of the fleshy hard drive brain.

Through functional brain-computer tomography, neuroscientists have been able to identify the various parts of the brain that are believed to be responsible for thought, memory, speech, and even emotion; however, the human mind is yet to be discovered in the brain. Intangible concepts such as understanding, judgment, personality, identity, and wisdom can not be found in images of functioning brain matter.

If we cannot see it, how might one then go about exploring the human mind? The basic premise of psychoanalysis is again like an iceberg, whose volume underwater is much greater than the volume above water. Similarly, our subconscious is much greater than our conscious awareness. Thus, to truly understand why we behave the way we do, it is necessary to tap into our subconscious and gain conscious awareness of our subconscious emotional and cognitive processes. Freud explained that such processes consist of various defense mechanisms, which are automatic forms of response to situations that arouse unconscious emotions. Through what has become known as psychoanalysis, Freud would essentially dig into his client's distant past to explain their near past. And then, with a greater understanding or conscious awareness of such past behaviors, one may then use this higher level of awareness to breakdown maladaptive defense mechanisms, stop transference behaviors, prioritize core desires, question and test core beliefs, and establish a healthier identity.

While Psychoanalysis is very intriguing and interesting and has found a solid theoretical basis, in practice, psychoanalysis is a very long and difficult process, which does not have an extremely high success rate of only about 55%; and, this number was much lower for personality disorders (de Maat et al. 2009). Thus, while it may be helpful to discuss and identify one's problems, change has to take place in the present if it is to occur at all. Take, for example, a person with a drinking problem. They can explore their past and find relevant explanations for their drinking problem, which may help them find new strength to change their drinking habits. But when it comes down to it, it is the drink that this person does not drink, from moment to moment, day for day, in the here and now that leads to a behavior change. As such, the past cannot change the future; only the present can change the future.

Thus if you are interested in gaining an understanding of why you may behave the way you do, then psychoanalysis can be very helpful in gaining such an understanding. However, that understanding does not automatically transform directly into a changing of the behavior itself. In addition to this, such an understanding could also lead to a rationalization of the problem, which could, in turn, lead to a justification of the behavior. For example, if one comes to the understanding that one's aggressive communication is a result of the necessity to defend oneself in childhood, rather than changing this behavior, one could conclude that this is simply how they are and everybody else should have to deal with it. Sure, such a rationalization could offer some significant relief to the problem but does little to change the behavior that leads to the problem.

While the technique of psychoanalysis is long, complex, and difficult, the psychology of God, with respect to the past and past behaviors, is extremely simple and almost too good to be true. In Romans 8:38-39, Paul suggests that the only thing that can come between God and us is our past. However, as I will point out later, focusing on the past does little if anything towards changing future behaviors. Thus, one should take care not to "conform to the pattern of this world, but be transformed by the renewing of your mind. Then you will be able to test and approve what God's will is – His good, pleasing, and perfect will" (Romans 12:2). In contrast to the prayer of salvation, which is a conscious decision that needs to be made only once in a lifetime, the renewing of the mind is something that has to be prayed for and meditated upon daily, with great concentration, dedication, and motivation.

In addition to the various concepts of the mind that have been thus far discussed, one could include discussions about personality, identity, attitude, and many more such psychological constructs that lie outside my field of expertise. In addition to this, I could, and I will insert here, an entire book on the mind of God as described in the Holy Scriptures, giving a new perspective on the idea of man being created in God's image. 1. Paul illustrated the complexity of the human mind regarding theological and metaphysical constructs. Matters of this nature are often unfalsifiable. And, although science has found ways to measure specific aspects of the mind, an accurate measure of the human mind on the level described in 1 Cor. 2:10-16. Thus, this topic will be reserved for my next book.

Instead, I would like to discuss an aspect of the human mind that has received a great amount of scientific attention. The concept of humor is a tribute to the human mind. I define humor as the ability to view a situation from numerous perspectives. With humor, the human mind displays its presence, making sense of things that make no sense through association, intuition, and blindsight.

Life Stress and Humor

Stress and humor are two examples of concepts that are primarily registered in the mind. The term stress originally comes from the field of physics and is used to quantify the strength of a material construction under static friction, which is another term for pressure. The term stress has also been used to describe the many different aspects of life, which can weigh down on an individual, causing them to collapse under life's pressure. In both psychology and physics, an even distribution of pressure has been found to enable a structure or an individual to withstand greater amounts of stress. Carefully calculated architecture is sufficient to construct a building or a bridge so that it will be able to withstand an expected amount of stress. However, if the building or bridge is exposed to an unexpected amount of stress, the structure will fall. The construction of a human being is vastly more complicated than anything built by humans, but the very same principles apply.

The stress that humans have to endure is also much more complicated than physical weight. Furthermore, while in the world of physics, unexpected stress, like an airplane crashing into a skyscraper, is truly unexpected, in life, one can and should expect unexpected stress. Hence the worldwide saying, shit happens. As such, a carefully calculated architecture may not be enough to keep an individual from collapsing at times of great and unexpected stress. But we are fortified with something that no other building or bridge has. We have humor. And with humor, our minds can choose to perceive a situation and, through humor, perceive and compare various perspectives.

I stated previously that I was given two years to live when I was first diagnosed with MD. That, of course, crushed me. It crushed my heart, body, mind, and soul. During all that unexpected stress, I had a flashback memory at a church summer camp. Being from a strong Christian family and having a famous father, I did not get much attention at such camps. The church leaders spent all their time with kids who needed their help and left me to fill up 1000 water balloons for all the other kids to play with while the other kids on the work crew and I cleaned the kitchen after lunch. On the last evening, just before the typical alter call, they brought an older kid up on stage. He was the coolest kid there. He played guitar in the band, had a tattoo, and long hair. Everyone thought he was so awesome. He went up on stage and told the story about how he tried to kill himself by drinking laundry detergent only a couple of months previously, but now he has given his life to Christ. While everyone cheered, and all the girls wanted to hug him, and all the leaders wanted to give him a high five; I could not help to think, "Idiot, do you know how much laundry detergent you have to drink before it will kill you and how long that will take?!?!" The truth was this kid was clearly not on track, bad grades, a sinful lifestyle, no accomplishments to speak of, yet he was the cool one, the hero of the youth group?!?! So with that in my mind, we were all sent out to go off alone and think about if we wanted to accept Christ into our lives. I had done that probably 20 times by then and had come to the clear understanding that you only have to do it once. So I wanted to talk to God about this. I asked God, "Why is my life so perfect, what kind of testimony will I ever be able to give? When will I ever be able to tell how God got me through an impossible problem when I never have any problems?" That is when I heard God laugh and say, do not worry; you will get your chance.

This memory flashed into my mind as I laid in my hospital bed after receiving that diagnosis and death sentence. The irony of the memory made me burst into laughter. This confused the nurses, who were respectfully ignoring my crying just moments before my laugh attack, which made me laugh even more. They thought I had lost my mind at that moment; when it was at that moment, I had actually found it, which led me to more laughter. Through all this laughter, I could not help but to think, "Muscular Dystrophy, bring it on. Bitch!"

Humor has been documented as a source of enjoyment in the earliest manuscripts (Wild, Rodden, Grodd, & Ruch, 2003). From a humorous perspective, Joseph's story, which has the tone of a Shakespeare's comedy only, it was much more ado about something, rather than nothing (Gen.

50:20). I do not think it is hard for one to understand Abraham's and Sarah's impulse to laugh at the news that they will bear a child at the ripe old age of 90 and 99 years old (Gen. 17:17; 18:12). And, I particularly enjoy reading Elisha's humorous taunts towards the Prophets of Baal. As they dance and cut themselves, trying to get Baal to respond, Elisha taunts them, suggesting that Baal may be on the toilet taking a dump. Most translations state, "maybe he is deep in thought," but Elisha's taunt was somewhat deeper if you look at the original Hebrew (1 Kings 18: 27). Indeed, due to the seriousness of the subject matter, the humor in the Bible often goes undetected, but it is there quite plainly. In my opinion, Jesus was making a hilarious joke when he told his disciples to throw their fishing nets on the other side of the boat. He even did what is referred to as a 'call back' in stand up comedy when he unexpectedly made the same joke again in John 21:5, after His resurrection. In fact, it was due to this absurd quip that the disciples recognized that it was Jesus.

It has been said of God, in various contexts, that God has a sense of humor. The profoundness of this idea is not so obvious. To realize this, one has to appreciate how cognitively complex the concept of humor is (Matin, 2007; Ruch, 1998). While it has been recorded that other animals may laugh in response to emotionally provocative stimuli, only humans have been known to use humor actively as a coping method. The fact that humor has been proven to be an effective coping method is evidence of the mind's existence above and beyond the brain (Kolb 2013). For there is no logical, chemical, or physical way, in which laughing about something should make that something not only seem less threatening but also be scientifically proven as such (Matin, 2007; Ruch, 1998). Thus, the topic of humor is a perfect example of the depth of the human mind.

The popular assumption that "laughter is the best medicine" or, as equally often assumed, "humor is the best medicine" has motivated a great amount of research. And indeed, empirical studies have shown that individuals were less sensitive to pain under' humorous' conditions than they were under control conditions (Zweyer et al., 2004). Nevertheless, overall, humor research results offer little gained knowledge above and beyond that which the popular assumption presumes (Nezlek & Derks, 2001; Nezu, Nezu, & Blissett, 1988; Kuiper & Nicholl 2004; Kuiper, Grimshaw, Leite, and Kirsh 2004).

The sense of humor may be defined as the ability to view a situation from various perspectives. Scientifically observed behaviors have measured coping humor, humor in social circles, humor appreciation, humor production, and humor as a personality trait. I have also suggested that the definition of a sense of humor should not involve the associated themes of laughter nor degrees of funniness as it usually is in the field of scientific psychology. Much of the previous humor research indirectly supports this proposed definition of a sense of humor (Kolb, 2013); however, Ritchie (2004) seems to directly support this notion and explained that jokes build upon the audience's interpretation or viewpoint of the set-up. Next, the punch-line forces the audience to perceive a different interpretation from the set-up.

Take, for example, this simple joke. Customer: "I'd like to try on that dress in the window." Salesperson: "Well, if you really want to, but we do have dressing rooms." In terms of perspectives, the set-up, and the punch line's unexpected viewpoint, it is clear what the customer meant, and still, the salesperson's answer is also valid. It is the perception of the possible perspectives that make any joke or situation funny. One might perceive a perspective that a customer might try on a dress in a sales window or that this woman might not know what a dressing room is or the salesman's shameful suggestion. In addition to this, as one reads this joke, one unconsciously visualizes this situation and fills in the blanks with additional circumstances. For example, this joke offers no information about the woman's attractiveness. Still, a male reader may find himself imagining an attractive woman, while a female listener may find herself imagining a lecherous salesman. The salesperson may also be unconsciously visualized as the typical "dumb blond" or the "stuck up" cheerleader type. The possibilities are immense. Therefore, it may be suggested that someone with a greater sense of humor can perceive a situation from many various perspectives. In comparison, someone with a lower sense of humor can perceive the same situation from fewer perspectives.

This would clearly explain Freud's opinion of humor as the most effective coping method (Führ & Martin, 2002; Kuiper & Martin, 1993). People who use humor as a coping method can perceive a stressful situation from various other perspectives rather than just a stressful perspective. The process of humor coping is then closely related to the process of understanding the perspectives of a joke, as previously discussed.

Essentially, our sense of humor applies the concept of set-up and punch-line to stressful situations. It redistributes the pressure over the whole body rather than on only once a critical point. This allows the mind, heart, body, and soul time to regain momentum. For example, a person who faces a very real and stressful situation is the set-up. If this person is then able to find a perspective of this stressful situation, which is plausible yet amusing, then this will become a punch line. Through the perception of this alternative perspective, they may suddenly experience the feeling of mirth. They may even laugh, but that is not what is important. Rather, the stressful pressure must be no longer concentrated on a single point but instead spread out evenly over their entire construction. Then with newly and evenly distributed pressure, one is better able to withstand the pressure of unexpected stressful events.

Perceiving and presenting humorous perspectives is both a skill and a talent. For some individuals, this seems to come naturally; for others, it is more difficult. Nevertheless, this skill can be learned and improved. This does not mean anyone can learn to be a professional comedian. Nevertheless, I would suggest that everyone can improve their ability to perceive situations from a humorous perspective with the right training. That is, one can improve one's sense of humor. This implies that people, who do not instinctively successfully use humor as a coping strategy, or humor in social environments, or in other areas of life, can learn and improve their humor skills through exercises adopted from the performing arts, in which one learns to become more aware of the various possible perspectives of a situation.

The Human Soul

To love God and others with all of our soul means to strive to do good and become righteous through our deeds (Psalms 11:7), although this is essentially impossible Romans 3:23. Nevertheless, the effort and striving of righteousness are important for our spiritual growth here on earth, but not for our salvation. "For it is by grace, you have been saved, through faith – and this is not from yourselves, it is the gift of God (Ephesians 2:8). That is, there is nothing at all we can do to gain God's love; we have it because He has given it to us freely. But, it is through our deeds, actions, and behaviors, in that we try to be righteous, that we demonstrate our love for Him.

The fourth source of impulse is from the soul, which is equally elusive as the mind. Previously, I referred to the soul as the sub-conscious self-awareness, which is a very broad and generic term. This simply means that we are not consciously aware of our soul, but it still is a big part of who we are as individuals. Although this is an accurate description, it is not a very helpful one. Because if we are not aware of our soul, how can we discuss it and think about it and learn and grow with it? It is not so easy.

Like the mind, the soul is an abstract unit that one can neither see nor touch, but it is nevertheless a unique component to every person. The soul may also be compared to Freud's concept of the superego, which Freud described as the motivation or drive to fill one's own needs, but in a way that coincides with one's morals. According to Freud, the superego develops after the ego, which is the drive to fulfill one's needs but without the consideration for moral. A while back, I came across a flowery Facebook Mem. It was titled Ego vs. Soul and made the following comparisons:

The ego seeks to serve itself, the soul seeks to serve others.

The ego seeks outward recognition, the soul seeks inner authenticity.
Ego sees life as a competition, soul sees life as a gift.
Ego seeks to preserve self, soul seeks to preserve others.
Ego looks outward, soul looks inward.
Ego feels lack, soul feels abundance.
Ego is mortal, soul is eternal.
Ego is drawn to lust, soul is drawn to love.
Ego seeks wisdom, soul is wisdom.
Ego enjoys the prize, soul enjoys the journey.
Ego is cause to pain, soul is cause of healing.
Ego rejects God, soul embraces God.
Ego seeks to be filled, soul is eternal wholeness.
Ego is me, soul is we.

Thus, when we talk about someone being a generally good or bad person, we are discussing their soul. Are they generally motivated to do good, or are they generally motivated to do bad by some standard? In this respect, the soul is equivalent or at least associated with our morals, a description, or a measure of our goodness. How eager are we to help as opposed to how easy it is for us to turn away and not help.

Finally, if our identity is a description of who we are, then our soul is a description of whom we want to become. This would correspond to the belief, which is common across many religions, that the soul is eternal. One does not even have to adhere to religious theology to assert that if there is life after death, then our bodies do not continue, at least not in the form in which we would have left them: dead. Otherwise, we would all be zombies in the afterlife. If one assumes that the afterlife is good, then our hearts, which are often broken in this life, will be significantly changed. Likewise, our minds will be significantly changed because our distorted core beliefs will be rectified as well as the things we ponder about, such as God and Heaven. Therefore, from the process of elimination, if we are in any way the same 'person' in Heaven that we are on earth, this sameness will have to be a continuation of our soul because everything else will be significantly changed. Thus, the concept of the soul exists in many beliefs, which makes it all the more difficult to define.

While impulses from the soul are difficult to define, when one experiences such an impulse, then it becomes apparent. This is the kind of impulse that inspires explanations of behaviors such as, "A man's gotta do, what a man's gotta do." Or, "it just feels like the right thing to do." But, such an impulse is more than just a feeling; it is a conviction. If one suppresses an impulse out of the body, one is likely to miss an opportunity to act. If one suppresses in impulse out of the mind, one only postpones the action. If one suppresses an impulse out of the heart, it may affect one's mood. But, if one suppresses an impulse out of the soul, it may leave a lasting effect that one will carry with them until it is somehow resolved. Impulses out of the soul are not very common, but they are extremely powerful.

I differentiate clearly between what I refer to as the soul and what I refer to as the spirit. What I am referring to is that which is contained in the bounties of the human body and represents the needs, wants, and deepest desires of the individual. If the mind contains the person's identity, who they think they are, the identity of the soul is then whom they want to become. As such, the soul may also be described in terms of one's purpose in life. This soul that I am speaking of is a part of the human and thus cannot somehow float away, as the spirit is often believed to be able to do.

Many people confuse the soul with the spirit. In my interpretation, the soul is distinctly different from the spirit, in that the soul is a part of the person, while the spirit is not. This is illustrated most obviously through our grammatical language. When we discuss spirit, it is most often followed by the preposition 'of': A spirit of... Secondly, a spirit is something that we adopt. One can adopt the spirit of God, or of the night, of nature, of the wild, of whatever one wants to identify with.

Thus the spirit that one adopts is essentially a decision of the person, not a part of the person that has been developing with the person since conception. Finally, it is thoroughly conceivable that two people may have the same spirit. Students are said to have school spirit, not different schools, but the same school. The term goth may be used to describe a group of people who embrace the spirit of darkness, not different darknesses, like dark chocolate, dark skin, but rather one and the same understanding of darkness. 2. Tim. 1:7 illustrates this perfectly, "For God hath not given us the spirit of fear; but of power, and of love, and of sound mind." Here, we clearly see the spirit is not from us, in terms of a part of our development, but something we adopt, which also implies that we have to accept it. This is the King James version, which uses the preposition 'of' to describe what kind of spirit it is. And, this same spirit is offered to each of us. Thus, we can all have this same spirit.

The soul, on the other hand, can not be described as the spirit has above. It would sound weird to say someone has the soul of ... whatever. The soul is not something that we choose to adopt at some point, but rather it develops within us, not exactly through our experiences, but rather through our reactions, thoughts, and emotions towards our experiences. Finally, each individual has a unique and individual soul.

I would suggest that the most accurate description or synonym for one's soul is one's moral, as in 'old King Cole was a jolly ol' soul, and a jolly ol' soul was he." Thus, I would suggest, the soul is a linear spectrum of good vs. bad. Evidence of this can be found in the fact that many very good people do not have the Holy Spirit. I know Mormons, Muslims, Buddhists, Hindus, and atheists who are very nice and good people who love their neighbors. Still, they do not have the Spirit of God, which only comes through Jesus. As such, the spirit is a fifth element that is not confined in the heart, body, mind, and soul but flows through each of these and beyond, and longs to connect with God, or rather a god. For we are all slaves to something, and that something for which we live. As such, there is no such thing as atheism. Atheism claims there is no creator, but they, like everyone else, have a core desire, what they live for, what they want, their heart's desire, be it money, power, success, love, peace, whatever. Humans cannot, not want. The desire to not want anything is a desire in itself, which essentially pulls the rug out from under Buddhism, which teaches that one reaches enlightenment by ridding oneself from all desires.

The soul, abstract as it is, may also be perceived rather simply on a binary variable, good or bad. Kohlberg attributed the term moral in this context and developed a model of moral development, which we previously discussed. Kohlberg noticed that people often do the right thing but for very different reasons; and that the reasons we have for doing the right thing are based on a six-stage development process, in which each reason could be described as nobler as the previous.

One's moral development furthers building a unique personality in that moral development is a major part of the self-identification process, which is unique to human beings. That is, animals, unless their behavior has been learned and influenced by humans, do not behave good or bad, but rather purely instinctively. When a lion kills an antelope, he is not doing it to be evil or mean, but rather simply following his drives and instincts. He does not question whether or not his actions are right or wrong. On the other hand, humans have the capacity to make judgments about right and wrong and have the motivation to act accordingly (Broderick & Blewitt, 2006).

CHAPTER THREE

Models of Development

In any psych. 101 course, the following models of development are likely to be addressed. In most cases, such models are conveyed to illustrate that the development occurs in plateau-like stages, in which, at some point, a child reaches the next stage and remains on that stage until the next stage is reached. However, such illustrations are misleading. Development does not occur in plateau-like increments but rather gradually, linearly, and fluctuating. That is, a child does not simply suddenly reach the next stage of development never to return, but rather the stages tend to flow into one another gradually. Thus, they should not be viewed as a checklist to foster development but rather as a very general map that may be used to identify where each individual child is in each of their various developmental processes. In the long run, (that being adulthood), it is not completely essential that each child reach a certain stage by a certain age. As such, developmental models merely illustrate the chronological order of commonly observed behaviors as they relate to various aspects of development.

Freud's Model of Sexual Development

Freud's model of sexual development is based on his theory that each person's personality is comprised of three distinct aspects of personality: the id, the ego, and the superego. Each of these three develops in turn and is in conflict with the others, particularly during development. The

Id represents the biological self and is the first to develop. The Id serves to fulfill the biological needs of the individual through instincts and drives. As a child's identity begins to develop, with sufficient cognitive and physical abilities, the ego eventually sets in and begins regulating the Id. Where the Id only merely wants to fulfill needs, the ego considers how these needs may best be met by appropriate or inappropriate means as determined by society. As such, the Id tells us what we want, and the ego tells us how we should go about getting it in terms of effectiveness. The third component, the superego, is sometimes referred to as the 'internalized parent.' It is a result of the conflict between the id and the ego. Where the Id tells you what you want and the ego tells you how to get it, the superego outweighs the two, as it is often portrayed as a little angel sitting on one shoulder and a little devil sitting on the other.

For example, when a baby wants something, it does what it can to get it. But, since it is a baby, all it can do is cry, so it cries. It does not think about if this is the best means of getting what it wants. It does not think about who, if anyone, even hears the crying. It just cries and does not stop until it gets what it wants, relentlessly. In a few years, that will change. At about the age of 4, a child will still cry to get what it wants, but it does so on a higher level of conscious awareness. If the child is outside playing and hurts himself, he will probably start crying because his Id will tell him he needs help. But if he then realizes that no one hears him crying, his ego will tell him this is not working. So, he will get up, go back inside the house. During this time, he may even stop crying and appear to be perfectly fine until he knows that someone will hear him, and then he will start crying again. If his mom is on the phone just then, that will not matter to him at all; he will just keep crying. And if he does not think she is responding fast enough, he will start crying louder or may even start throwing stuff, or in some way escalate his attempts to gain the attention he wants. Not, for a moment will he stop and think, "Oh, mom seems to be on the phone now with an important call, I will just be quiet now, I am sure she will attend to my need of a band-aid, as soon as she is able." Over time the child's ego will figure out the most effective ways to get what they want. Note, the ego works out the most effective ways, not the most appropriate ways.

Much later, after many interrupted phone calls, the child's superego will begin to regulate the id and the ego, based on past experiences. If the child has learned that interpreting his mother's business calls generally leads to negative responses from his mother, then he will eventually stop doing it. Even though the id tells him that he is hungry, and his ego tells him to get his mom to fulfill that desire, his superego may tell him that if he starts to throw a fit, his mom will most likely say, in a stern and consequent voice, "I will make dinner when I am done," which is more likely to consist of vegetables and less likely to consist of ice cream. Thus, he may decide a better course of action would be to simply go to the icebox get an ice cream himself. He may even take it quietly to his mom, who is on the phone, show her the ice cream, put on his best puppy dog face, give his mom a thumbs up, and hope for one in return.

Reiss (2000) has outlined the 16 basic desires that all humans have, to varying degrees: Power, Independence, Curiosity, Acceptance, Order, Saving, Honor, Idealism, Social contact, Family, Status, Vengeance, Romance (sex), Eating, Physical Exercise, and Tranquility. Although Freud tended to focus only on sex as the main drive with which an individual's id, ego, and superego had to deal with, it is easy to see, as, in the above example, sex is not the only drive-in which the id, ego, and superego regulate behavior. Nevertheless, Freud's model of development focuses exclusively on the development of sexual desires. For this reason, Freud's work has been considered outdated and overtly narrow-minded (Gilligan, 1982).

Freud's stages of development are named after the typical behaviors children to demonstrate at each stage. Babies are all about their mouths, and toddlers are all about their buts and kaka diapers. Later they discover their genitals. While Freud's sex and gender-driven model of development has since then been deemed narrow-minded (Gilligan, 1982), the concept of the id, the ego, and the superego, still has merit in explaining behavioral development. In the Oral stage of development, the ego and the superego have not yet developed. Thus the id is unhampered, and the baby instinctively does what it needs to do in order to get what it wants. During the anal stage, the superego develops, which begins what is commonly known as the terrible twos. At this point, the child begins to understand right from wrong and knows he should simply wait until his mom has a moment to lift him out of his high chair. But the toddler, still primarily driven by the id, will swipe his plate and remaining contents from the table to express that he has had enough of the delicious meal made with love and wants down out of his chair right now. According to Freud, no amount of scolding or reprimand will lead a child to understand that such table manners are inappropriate until the superego is developed. But even then, if doing what wrong leads to what the toddler wants is, the toddler's id and ego will conflict until the superego develops and begins to intermediate in the Phallic and Latency stages. During these stages, concepts such as identity, personality, and core beliefs come into play and continue to develop into adulthood.

Stage	Age	Behavior
Oral	0-1	Pleasure is experienced through the mouth and so babies put everything they can in their mouths.
Anal	1-3	The anal region becomes a significant source of pleasure. The exploration of objects occurs with the hands rather than the mouth.
Phallic	3-6	The genital region becomes a significant source of pleasure. Behavior corresponding to the Oedipus Complex may occur.
Latency	6-15	Personality development begins to take root in work and play.
Genital	15- Adult	Puberty. Sexual drives become a significant source of motivation.

Piaget's Model of Cognitive Development

Piaget's theory of cognitive development consists of four stages: Period of Sensory-Motor, Period of Pre- Conceptual Thought, Period of Intuitive Thought, and Period of Concrete Operations. The period of sensory-operations actually begins even before birth. During this stage, a baby demonstrates innate reflexes to stimuli. For example, a baby will turn its head toward a light source. Even while still in the womb, a baby will recognize his mother's voice. It will suck on anything that touches its mouth, and it will project experienced emotion through facial expressions. Incidentally, the sense that develops first, and is arguably the most important, is the sense that is very often forgotten (Pope & Whiteley, 2003). Humans have six, not five senses. The sense of balance is extremely important for early cognitive development (Blythe, 2000). If we did not have a sense of balance, then we would not be able to navigate through gravity. But as it is, a baby, before it knows anything else in the world, it knows the difference between up and down and arranges itself, it a head-down position when it is ready to be born. Blythe (2000) then illustrated that through the sense of balance, all the crawling, falling, and eventually walking do not only foster movement skill but also get our two brain halves working together. When we begin to fall to the left, the right side of the body has to react. Through the struggle against gravity, the right/left brain hemisphere communication is fostered, which has been found to be directly associated with later reading, writing, and concentration skills (Warner- Rogers et al., 2000).

The beginning of speech marks the beginning of the period of pre-conceptual thought. It is at this time that a child begins to arbitrarily use symbols in the form of language. During this period, it is common for a child to say dog when he sees one, but also might say dog when he sees any four-legged animal. When thought begins to become independent of perception, this marks the beginning of the period of intuitive thought. A child will now understand that rows of five red chips and five blue chips have the same number of chips regardless of how the chips are lined up. That is, the laws of conservation and object permanence begin to be recognized. The recognition of all the laws and properties of conservation and continuity marks the beginning of the final period of concrete operations.

Stage	Age	Behavior
Sensorimotor	0 – 2	At first, stimuli trigger reflexive behavior, which eventually induces representational thought.
Preoperational Thought	2 – 7	Representational thought is simple, focusing on only one piece of information at a time. The thought process is not yet logical.
Concrete Operational Thought	7 – 12	Thinking becomes more rapid and efficient. Logical thought processes can 'connect the dots'.
Formal Operational Thought	12 – Adult	Logical thinking abilities extend to abstract thinking abilities.

According to Piaget, a child cannot learn tasks that are outside of his stage of cognitive development. Thus, there is no point in trying to teach a child something that it can not yet learn because the child simply lacks the necessary cognitive skills. That is, no one who can not yet add 2+2 will have any chance of learning calculus. As such, Piaget's theory of cognitive development has become a guiding principle that parents should not press their children too hard; they will learn it when they are good and ready. While this is true, I would argue that other channels through which children learn are not confined by cognitive abilities, such as motor skills.

Models of Development

I began teaching each of my children chess as soon as they stopped putting everything in their mouths (ca. 18 months), but I broke it down into very small steps based on simple visual and motor skills. First, they learned to separate the black pieces from the white pieces, then the pawns from the other pieces, then they learned to pair the rooks, knights, and bishops, and then they learned to differentiate between the king and the queen. After they could do this, they learned to set up the pawns in a row and the back row in pairs from the outside in, and finally, they learn the association: white queen, white square, black queen, black square. These are all visual learning behaviors that require only preoperational thought. After that, I began teaching the children the first ten opening moves for black again various white attacks. Of course, they had no understanding of the complexities of chess at this young age. Their chess playing behavior was only learned motor behavior, no different than a child pointing to a duck in response to the question, "where is the duck" or learning the hand movements to 'itsy bitsy spider.' While this is still a long way from chess, by the time Lucy was three, she knew the correct responses to about ten different chess openings and could play out the first ten moves. It looked like she was playing chess, but she was not. She still did not have the cognitive abilities to understand how each of the pieces moved and worked together to form a checkmate. All she could do was set up the chessboard and perform the motor sequences of various openings. None of this learning did anything to increase or speed up her cognitive abilities. So was it a waste of time? Certainly not; we had fun eating snacks and "playing chess," she certainly enjoyed the attention she got from others when she demonstrated her 'chess ability.' In this video, she is not yet three, has no idea what she is doing, but goes through the moves of the Spanish open like a pro: https://www.youtube.com/watch?v=5WdcOkeXj1g.

However, when she entered into the concrete operational thought stage and began to understand how the pieces move and work together to form a checkmate, she did not have to learn the opening principles.

They were already embodied in her visual and motor skills. It was as if her brain only had to learn, what hands, fingers, and arms already knew. Thus, through the early visual and motor exercises, she acquired an opening repertoire before she could understand the principles of a chess opening. Thus, I would agree with Piaget that a child's cognitive development will run its course, and there is little that one can do on a cognitive level to foster this development. Still, motor, visual, and verbal imitation skills also offer much learning potential upon which one can build.

Erikson's Model of Social-Emotional Development

Development implies change, and change is often associated with struggle; thus, many of the various models of development are marked by diverse aspects of status. The concept of status is a means by which humans and other vertebrates express their emotional communication in reaction to emotionally provoking stimuli. When we perceive something that evokes emotion, our body reacts in the form of emotional communication (aka. Body language) in response to counteract the stimulus. That is, when we are suddenly startled, we assume a defensive stance; when we are suddenly surprised with flowers, we assume an accepting stance (unless we do not like the person, in which case our status in terms of emotional expression will project that as well). In any case, our status, defined through our mimic, posture, gesture, action, and voice, is constantly changing and reacting to any and all emotionally provoking stimuli (EPS). Like a kind of friction between ourselves and our environment, our status is constantly adapting and changing in response to the various EPS we are constantly encountering; this generally happens outside our cognitive awareness (Kolb, 2010, 2017; Bucci, 1995; Johnstone, 1981).

Although he never directly addressed the concept of status in his model of psychosocial development, Erikson acknowledged the presence of an ever-existing struggle, similar to the kind of friction associated with the concept of status, during the stages of social-emotional development. Each of Erikson's stages is defined through the struggle of one human quality versus another. For example, in the first stage of development, trust versus mistrust, a baby expresses its trust and mistrust directly through status as a reflection of its emotional state. That is, a baby may cry in the arms of a stranger but smile in the arms of its mother. One could argue that each of Erikson's stages is marked by a significant change in a person's status as they develop from one stage to the next throughout their lifetime. Erikson stated that "as long as the establishment of identity is incomplete a crisis exists which ... amounts to an identity confusion" (as cited in Cote, 2006).

It is not difficult to imagine the various changes in status that a child might project as it reaches each stage for the first time. For example, in the autonomy vs. shame stage, a child will, for the first time, let go and walk free-handed. Youtube is full of videos of proud babies, who radiate with pride as they realize they are walking like mom and dad, just before they fall again and go boom. Once a child has experienced a significant degree of success in a skill, it is in their consecutive attempts that the struggle between autonomy and shame becomes apparent; doubt and determination flash back and forth in their face and bodily expression.

Our previous example of the child who wants ice cream, but knows better than to disturb his mom on the phone to ask for it, is also a good example of the initiative vs. guilt stage. The child inherently knows that the icebox, where the ice cream is kept, is a sort of sacred treasure chest. He knows there are good things in there, but he also knows he is probably not allowed to just get them himself. Or is he? What will happen if he does? His initiative will be rewarded with ice cream, but a consequence may very well follow. Is it worth the risk? There is only one way to find out.

Have you ever heard a child scream, "I can do it myself!!!" That is the calling call of the industry vs. inferiority stage. This right of passage is so common that more illustration is probably not at all needed.

Instead of an illustrated example, just reflect on something you have broken out of frustration because you could not get it to work right. Are you thinking about something in your childhood, or did something like this happen just this week? This might be a good time to point out that while most of us regress to previous stages of development from time to time, thorough out our lives.

Identity vs. Confusion is also a stage of social-emotional development, to which even adults often regress. However, primarily it is a struggle that begins around puberty. The central question around this struggle is, "Who are you?" In a struggle to fit in somewhere, teenagers often oscillate between whom they think they are and who they think they want to be until the storm eventually settles. However, even in adult life, dramatic situations can arise, which unleash the storm of confusion and identity from time to time. On an interesting side note, Carrol Gilligan (1982) found that males defined their identity primarily in terms of what they do, while females defined their identity in terms of their relationships.

After we have figured out who we are, or at least narrowed it down significantly, an individual will ultimately begin to ask themselves, who might be a good match for me. This stage is not the introduction of one's romantic dating life, but more likely, it is the end of one's romantic dating life. Relationships mean sharing, but sharing is ultimately in conflict with instinctual self-preservation. Does one want to remain free or settle down? This is the basis of the struggle, but it also goes much deeper, because unlike all other social-emotional development struggles up until this point, one can not simply work out this struggle on their own. The struggle is not, simply, does one want a partner or not. But also, can one find a partner if one is wanted. Then is it the right partner? Is the desired partner available? Or is the other side of the coin the issue. What if one has a partner but would rather retain a significant amount of freedom. Or, one has a partner, but not the desired one. Does one compromise one's desires or hold out for a better match. Everyone knows this is a very stressful struggle. Buss (1999) outlined the instinctual drives behind mating and relationship, which I happened to had been studying as my last divorce was taking place. It made me want to regress back to the Industry vs. Inferiority stage and throw the book against the wall many times.

That which many have come to know as the midlife crisis, Erikson defined as the Generativity vs. Stagnation stage. This is the point in an individual's life when they ask themselves, "So, is this it? Is this all life has to offer, or can I maybe squeeze a little more out of it?" In the introduction sections of this book, I mentioned a few times that God has created me with a specific purpose. It is at this stage, whether one believes in God or not, that one inevitably asks themselves, was that my purpose or is it still to come? Even the renowned atheists Lawrence Krauss, whom I quoted earlier on page ten, admits that he desires to find purpose in his life, even though he does not believe that life itself has a purpose. Thus, whether one believes that God defines one's purpose in life, or whether one believes each person must define their own purpose in life, defining this purpose and achieving it is a very important matter. Viktor Frankl (1959), in his iconic book, *Man's Search for Meaning*, suggested that when one no longer finds any purpose in their life, death may very soon follow. I would agree with this but choose to focus on the other side of the coin. I would argue that joy, true enduring joy is not only a feeling but is a state of mind that comes from pursuing God's purpose in our lives. For if our ultimate goal is to, at one time, hear God tell us, "Well done, good and faithful servant." (Matt. 25:21). We pursue this goal to the best of our ability and capability during all the stages of our life's development, then come what may, the core of our hearts, will always be filled with joy.

Finally, the last of Erikson's stages is Integrity vs. Despair. At some point in my life, a long time ago, I began a birthday tradition. Every year on my birthday, I would find a quiet place and reflect upon my life and ask myself this question, "Am I satisfied with what I have achieved so far?" If my heart stopped beating at that moment, would my last thought be, "Wait, I'm not ready yet!" or would it be, "It is finished." (John, 19:30). It was only a couple of years ago that I heard of the idea of a "bucket list." It honestly took me a moment to grasp the concept because I have never waited very long to do that, which I felt I needed to do. I do not really have anything that I would want to put on my bucket list. Even if I rack my brain, I cannot think of anything I want to do before I die. Not because there is nothing I want to do, but because as soon as such an event comes to mind, it does not get put on a bucket list, it gets put on a to-do list, and it gets done. Sometimes I hear people say, If I had a million dollars, then I would (insert dream). Why wait? Anything you need a million dollars to do, you can start doing for zero dollars. For if it is God's will for you to do, whatever it is you have on your bucket list, then the money is not going to be an issue; just start doing it. And if it is not God's will for you to do, whatever it is you have on your bucket list, then just start doing it anyway, and He will redirect your heart and give you new desires if you are obedient to His Holy Spirit.

Stage	Age	Behavior
Trust vs. Mistrust	0 - 1	Hope – Infants develop trust for those who meet their needs or mistrust those who do not.
Autonomy vs. Shame	1 - 3	Will – Toddlers begin to want to do things for themselves or they doubt their abilities.
Initiative vs. Guilt	3 – 6	Purpose – Preschoolers want to initiate and complete tasks or feel guilty about their efforts.
Industry vs. Inferiority	6 – 12	Competence – Children gain pleasure in applying themselves or they feel inferior.
Identity vs. Confusion	12 - 20	Fidelity – Teenagers refine a sense of self or become confused about who they are.
Intimacy vs. Isolation	20 – 25	Love – Young adults struggle to form close relationships or they feel socially isolated.
Generativity vs. Stagnation	25 - 65	Care – People want to contribute to society or they feel a lack of purpose.
Integrity vs. Despair	65-death	Wisdom – Reflecting upon their lives, older adults may feel a sense of satisfaction or failure.

Erikson was a student of Freud, and, similar to Freud's Model of development, Erikson's model is also based on internal conflict. However, Erikson minimized the significance of the Id, being aware that we all have the same 16 basic desires: Power, Independence, Curiosity, Acceptance, Order, Saving, Honor, Idealism, Social Contact, Family, Status, Vengeance, Romance, Eating, Physical Activity, and Tranquility (Reiss, 2000). And although we each emphasize some basic desires more than others, it is a person's ego that determines which of these basic desires are more important and which are less important. Thus, Erikson's model focuses on the superego's rational processes, which are significantly associated with one's attitude and feelings towards the self and others.

Kohlberg's Model of Moral Development

Morality is a topic that has been highly debated between Christians and Atheists. Many Christians like to argue that the very fact that morality is a concept or issue at all is evidence that there is a God. For if there were no God that judges mankind in terms of sin versus righteousness, then we would have no concept of right and wrong. Therefore, because we have a concept of right and wrong, there must be a God that bestowed them upon us. That is, the very fact that humans are the only animals that, knowing right from wrong, are capable of sin, is explicit evidence of the story of Adam and Eve and the snake in the garden, which tricked Eve into eating the fruit of the tree of knowledge. While this is a good argument, many Christians go about presenting it the wrong way. They try to argue that God gave humans morality. And since only humans have morality, God exists. This argument is very easily shot down when one points out how immoral many proclaimed Christians are. The sex scandals of the catholic church alone offer sufficient counter-argument, without even mentioning wars and racisms. Then, having shot down the conclusion, the premise is left very much in doubt in the minds of many. With this momentum, atheists simply argue that human morality is simply a product of Darwinian evolution, just like our larger brains (Buss, 1999; Eccles, 1989). When this happens, we are no longer discussing the concept of morality, but rather the Darwinian evolution, which is already based on the assumption that there is no God. So neither side will accept the other side's arguments as valid and reliable. Thus rendering the discussion, while often entertaining, is most often pointless and unproductive.

The following thought experiment is perhaps a more effective argument. Mind you, this is only a thought experiment, and I am not at all suggesting that one should really perform this test because that would be inherently cruel. Imagine we caged 100 dogs, each in its own cage, and then someone tormented it with a stick over a significant period of time. After this period of cruelty, the door to the cage would be opened while the tormenter with the stick in his hand stood there in a neutral position. How many dogs would attack the man with the stick, how many would flee from the man with the stick, and how many would want to play fetch with the man and his stick? It seems practically inconceivable that any of the dogs would want to play and thus essentially forgive the man with the stick. The dogs would either attack the man, run away from him, or exhibit a submissive coweringly behavior. However, what if we did the same cruel thing with humans. Surely most would also either run away or attack, but with humans, it is thoroughly conceivable that some might forgive the individual and neither run nor attack. Not only is such a forgiving behavior conceivable, but history has also documented many such occurrences. A simple google search on "examples of forgiveness" will yield sufficient testimonies.

But what is morality, and where does it come from. In the previous chapter, I discussed the four components of the human: heart, body, mind, and soul. Each of these four components is intrinsically integrated. But, each goes through its own developmental process. Kohlberg's model of moral development is then essentially the development of the soul. When a child is firstborn, he or she has no concept of right or wrong; all it can do is follow his/her drives, instincts, and reflexes. However, eventually, a child will know right from wrong, and from that point on, the child will have to choose between the two. This is the struggle Freud described as a conflict between the id and the ego, but ultimately it is the person who is responsible and not the person's ego. If I get caught speeding, I will have little chance of getting out of the ticket by explaining it was not me; my ego was in such a hurry. Even if the cop writes out the ticket to Dr. Kolb's ego, it will be Dr. Kolb who has to pay for the ticket. Thus, Kohlberg cuts to the chase and examines why people choose to do the right thing over the wrong thing. This is a very interesting and inventive perspective because the formulation of the question in this manner avoids the question of what is right or wrong, which can easily lead to a pointless, endless, and unproductive discussion. As such, in a society with norms, why does any individual in that society follow and adapt to these norms, rather than just everyone doing only what they want to form their own subjective perspective? To answer this question, Kohlberg has outlined the motivations individuals have in doing what is right and discovered that these motivations change in a developmental pattern, to which humans adhere significantly.

Kohlberg explains the moral development of a person in six stages that he breaks up into three levels: Pre-conventional, Conventional, and Post-conventional. Each of these levels is broken down into two parts. However, for the sake of simplicity, we will just number them 1-6. A child's moral development begins with their understanding that their actions have consequences. This is something that, from a child's perspective, may come about rather suddenly. The first time a baby spits back out his mashed carrots and peas, his parents will probably say something sweet like, "oh, is your little tummy full? Did it bounce back out?" But there will come a day in which this and other such behaviors are no longer tolerated, and the child will suddenly be expected to behave in certain ways. Eventually, we want our children to become good little boys and girls, but why should they? What is in it for them? A child being fed his breakfast from his dad, wearing a white business shirt, will not think to himself, "Oh, dad has a white shirt on this morning, I better be careful not to spit my food at him, because he may have an important job interview, which may determine if he later has the means to put me through medical school so that I can later discover the cure for cancer, and offer it to society for free, which will then lead to worldwide unity and peace on earth for all mankind." No, that is not what he is thinking, but something like that would be the final stage of moral development.

Stage one of the moral development merely begins with the avoidance of scolding. Put a cookie on the table in front of a 3-year-old and tell her not to eat it. She probably will not eat it, as long as you are standing there watching her. She will not eat it because she does not want to get in trouble. However, if you leave the room, it may be as if you take the commandment with you. Now the child thinks the cookie is free game, as soon as there is no one there to scold. Kohlberg called this first stage the punishment and obedience orientation. During this stage, a child seems to only adhere to rules to avoid punishment, not because of his own personal judgment of right and wrong (Broderick & Blewitt, 2006).

Stage two is the concrete individualistic orientation. Characteristic of this stage is a child's tendency to follow the rules primarily to serve his own interests (Broderick & Blewitt, 2006). At this point, the child will have learned that scolding and punishment is not that much fun, but it is not that bad either. However, being deemed a good boy or girl definitely has its benefits. The child concludes that throwing his carrots on the floor is a fun game, but if he simply eats them upon request, he might get a cookie or something out of the deal. So, a child begins doing what is right and expected of him, not (only) to avoid punishment, but because he/she expect something in return. This can be a dangerous stage for parents because children may begin to extort all kinds of goods in return for good behavior. When exchanges like this become frequent, it may be time to introduce the next stage of moral development:

Parent: Put your legos in the box.
Child: No.
Parent: I said, put your legos in the box.
Child: I said, No. I do not want to.
Parent: Put your legos in the box, or you will go to bed early.
Child: Fine.
Parent: If you put your legos in the box, I will give you a cookie.

Child: I do not want a cookie. I want ice cream.
Parent: I do not have ice cream.
Child: Throws a fit, scattering the legos to every corner of the room.

At this point, the child is in charge. If the legos are now scattered all over the living room floor, and a prospective buyer is coming to view the house in 5 minutes, and then parents still need to frost the cupcakes or something. The parent can only either increase their offer or leave the legos on the floor and deal with the child later, and introduce the child to Kohlberg's third stage of moral development: social-relational perspective.

In this stage, helpfulness, generosity, and forgiveness become more important than self-interest. That is, an individual does what he is told to gain approval rather than material goods. After an event like the one scripted above, parents generally learn that it is not beneficial for any of the parties involved when parents get caught up in essentially paying their children for good behavior. It is at this point that good behavior begins to be expected as the norm. Rewards may follow excellent behavior, but good behavior is simply expected. With a significant amount of consequence on the side of the parents, the child will come to understand that being generally good in common everyday situations leads to a positive, comforting, and overall enjoyable relationship with the parents, while the opposite leads to animosity, stress, and discomfort. In this stage, altercations still occur, but the frequency and intensity will decrease as the child learns that being generally good keeps things running smoothly with mom and dad, which is more beneficial than extorting an ice cream when the opportunity arises.

The fourth stage is called the member- of- society perspective. During this stage, the social order becomes most important, as does the kind of behavior that contributes to society's functioning. After the child has experienced the benefits of being deemed "a good boy," the child will eventually begin to take pride in it. The child will have received compliments from distant family members, neighbors, teachers, etc., and will begin to feel good about being good and doing good things. A Christmas present will come from the neighbor so or so, and a plate of cookies also. Still, the real motivation of offering to take out the neighbor's trash is no longer what the child receives in material gains, or even the recognition of approval from the neighbors directly, but rather the recognition of himself ranked in society. The word gets around that that "Jimmy Smith" he is such a good kid. Through his good behavior, which now not only consists of doing what he is told but doing it before he is told, has earned him a good reputation in his environment.

At this point, a child does what he is told because he recognizes the importance of law and order. The child is no longer motivated solely by his desire to avoid punishment or receive material gain or recognition from his parents. In fact, the child can probably get an ice cream just about any time he wants just by asking a neighbor; and, he can also step out of line just about anytime he wants, without expecting too much of a reprimand, because his good deeds will have overshadowed his bad ones. However, this stage of moral development can also be very competitive. So in a family or neighborhood with a few children, tattle-telling can become an epidemic, as each child tries to gain the best standing in the immediate environment.

The fifth stage of moral development is the post-conventional level of the interpretation of law versus social contracts. Many people, even in adulthood, never reach these higher levels of moral development. During this phase, the social contract is valued over rules, laws, and norms. In this stage of moral development, one recognizes that it is not so much the law that is important, but the process and principles that they serve. An individual obeys laws, not for the sake of law, but because he recognizes the necessities that the law serves. For example, it is the law and a good one at that, that one should recognize the authority of the police. However, if one observes the police doing something they should not, then this law may be ignored because it is, at that moment, not serving the purpose it should. This is, of course, a situational judgment call. If I am speeding to McDonald's because I need to get there before they stop serving breakfast and a cop starts to chase me, and I continue racing to the drive-through, I will probably still get a ticket, and I probably would know and feel that I deserved to get a ticket. But, If I am racing someone to the hospital, who is very seriously hurt, and then a cop chases me, and I do not stop. I have still broken the law, the same as before, but this time I can feel justified in doing so.

In an infamous study, Milgram (1963) tried to show that the atrocities of the Holocaust came about because Germans have such high respect for law, order, and authority. And they do; it is amazing. We do not have many stop signs here because we have a rule that the car to the right has the right of way. Everyone knows that, and everyone follows that. If someone tries to cross the road at a pedestrian crossing while the light is red, even if there is no car in sight, someone will likely speak out and reprimand the person for not following the rules. In subway stations, there are no gates in which one has to put in a valid ticket to be able to pass through. One can simply board a train without a ticket, and only a very few do. But if they do and they get caught, they are chastised by the entire train compartment. Yes, the Germans love their rules and regulations to a ridiculous level of respect. In fact, I was declined a post-doc position because I had no documentation, which showed I had a particular level of English language skill. I tried to explain that English was my first language, and as such, I never studied it per se; I just grew up in Pittsburgh, PA, USA speaking English. But no, they wanted it on paper that somewhere at some time, I achieve a certain level of English language skill; otherwise, I was ineligible for the position.

Anyway, Milgram wanted to show that this sort of blind obedience to authority could not happen with intelligent Americans. He devised a test in which research subjects were required to administer increasingly stronger electric shocks to others, under the authority of a doctor, and with rational reasoning. He expected that these intelligent people would, at some point, refuse to continue administering the shocks (which were, of course, fake, but they did not know that). Surprisingly, all of the subjects continued administering the shocks they thought to be harmful, just because someone of greater authority told them to do it and stressed that it had to be done. This unequivocally demonstrated the power that authority has over our behavior and the difficulty one may have to resist it when the situation dictates that resistance to the authority of law is appropriate and necessary.

The sixth and last stage of Kohlberg's moral development is the universal ethical principles. At this phase, an individual's moral principles rise above specific laws, customs, and norms. This does not mean that laws, customs, and norms are no longer respected and followed, but it does mean that these man-made institutions are no longer the authority of dictating what right or wrong behavior is. In the previous stage, laws may be abandoned when they, in a particular situation, did not serve the necessity of the purpose they were created to serve. For example, the law that opposes speeding serves the purpose of keeping people safe; however, if I have someone in my car, who might die if I do not get them to the hospital as fast as possible, then in this particular situation, the law no longer serves the purpose it was intended to serve should. However, suppose a law, not only in a specific purpose but in its entirety, violates the higher principles of human rights. In that case, an individual, who lives by the higher principle of human rights, will disobey the law, not only in a specific situation but in general. Rosa Parks serves as a prime example of this. She concluded that the law that dictated that she should sit in the back of the bus violated human rights, not in a particular situation, but in general. Of course, such actions of civil disobedience are still subjected to popular opinion. One can debate whether Edward Snowden is a hero or a traitor, but one can not deny that he is a man who acts according to higher principles, regardless of whether or not one agrees with his principles. Whereas in the previous stage, one elects to momentarily break the law, in this stage, one elects to ignore the law, with the intention of challenging it.

Stage	Age	Behavior
Preconventional Level Punishment / Obedience	2-4	Punishment and Obedience. A child complies with rules to avoid punishment.
Preconventional Level Individual self-interest	4-7	A child complies with rules because he expects to be rewarded.
Conventional Level Social relational perspective	7-12	A child complies with rules to receive approval.
Conventional Level Member of Society	12-15	A child complies with rules because he recognizes the importance of law and order.
Postconventional Level Interpretation of Law	15-older	A person complies with rules because he values social contract.
Postconventional Level Universal ethics	Adulthood, if reached at all.	A person is less concerned with rules and laws but serves to meet a higher moral standard.

The importance of a caregiver to understand the process of moral development becomes apparent when a conflict arises through a child's challenge of authority. Consider a family with two children who are 10 - 11 years old, Bill and Sally. Let us assume that the family has the rule that Bill and Sally take turns cleaning up the dinner table, and let us assume that the children are in Kohlberg's fourth stage of moral development. Consider what might happen if it were Sally's turn to do the dishes, but that Sally was sick in bed with the flu. Bill's parents might then request that Bill then do the dishes. Bill might then protest, claiming that it would not be fair that he should have to do the dishes again, in which case he would technically be right because the rule dictates that Sally should do the dishes.

This is where many parents make the mistake of regressing back to the third stage of development, requesting that Bill be a good boy and do the dishes any way instead of allowing Bill to progress to the next stage of development by saying, "Bill, you are right it is not fair but Sally is sick and can not do the dishes; nevertheless, the dishes need to be done, and mom and dad have other things they have to do so the family is counting on him to pick up the necessary slack. However, let us assume that Bill's parents overlook this opportunity and request that Bill does the dishes simply to be deemed a good boy. Bill could then easily argue, "I did the dishes yesterday when it was my turn; therefore, I should already be deemed a good boy," and it is totally unfair to have to do them again to be given the appreciation that he already deserves. Bill then maintains, "No, I am not doing the dishes; it's not fair!" Bill's parents may then further regress to the next third stage of development: Individual Self-interest and offer Bill a prize for his compliance. "If you do the dishes, we will let you stay up 30 minutes later."

I trust you see where this is leading. If Bill now complies, he will have regressed in his moral development and perhaps demand prizes for future compliance for chores he should be doing simply because it is the family rule. However, let us assume that Bill does not comply, maintaining that he is being treated unfairly. That is, Bill remains at the fourth stage of moral development: Law and Order. Bill's parents are then likely to regress further in the stages of development and say, "If you do not do the dishes you will be grounded!" Thus, instead of fostering the child's moral development, the parents have done the exact opposite.

Whether or not you believe God bestowed upon humans to judge between right or wrong, or if you believe this attribute is a result of Darwinian evolution, the point that is relevant to Kohlberg's model of development is that, although humans can judge between right and wrong, this ability still needs to be developed properly through parenting. That is, children have the innate ABILITY to learn between right and wrong, but they still need to LEARN the difference between right and wrong.

This is essentially the difference between humans and all other animals. Humans, like all other animals, have drives, instincts, and reflexes that regulate their behavior. But only humans have the free will to override these innate forces and consciously choose between right and wrong.

God's Model of Character Development

Each of the various models of development previously discussed were developed through scientific psychology and focus on a specific aspect of child development. Next, I would like to suggest that a model of character development may be abstracted from the Holy Scriptures. In the Bible, humans are often referred to as the children of God. Furthermore, the Bible states that humans were made in God's image. Together these two statements shed new light and offer a new perspective in the discussion of child development. For if we are God's children, made in His image, and He is our heavenly Father, then the way he has raised us should offer an outline as to how we should raise our children.

The idea is a bit abstract yet quite simple. In this chapter, I would like to outline six distinct levels of character development that correspond to age stages used in the models previously discussed: Infancy (0-2), Toddler (2-4), Childhood 4-8, Adolescence (8-14), Young Adult (14-25), and Adult (25 and older). I would suggest that each of these stages corresponds to sections of the Bible.

Models of Development

Stage	Age	Bible Story
Infancy	0-2	Abraham to Joseph
Toddler	2-5	Moses to Joshua
Childhood	5-12	Joshua to David
Adolescence	12-18	Psalms, Proverbs, Job, and the Prophets
Young Adult	18-25	The Gospels
Adult	25 und older	Acts and Epistles

So if we are God's children made in His image, just as our children are to us, then the way He raised His children should offer some insight as to how we might raise our children. I can imagine that at this point, many readers may like to discard this book after reading the previous statement because the God of the Old Testament was harsh and perhaps even unjust at times. To this, I would like to make the following statement upfront. God did not give out participation trophies, and neither should we. And if you are a parent who thinks that one should not keep score at children's sporting events and that every child should get a trophy for everything they do, this should not be the only chapter you will not like in this book.

The simple fact of the matter is that God is not so terribly concerned with our happiness, but rather our growth. He has put us in an impossible situation that we can not navigate without His help. We have the free will to try it without his help, but we will certainly fail without Him. Now, some may claim that this is extremely unfair, but anyone that has acquired the ability to read this book will also have undoubtedly learned that life is simply harsh, unfair, and nobody gets through it alive. Indeed, life is deadly.

We bring children into this world, and we often take measures so that the child does not have to struggle with life's difficulties. This is now commonly referred to as lawnmower parenting, as opposed to the previous trend, helicopter parenting. In Helicopter parenting, the Parents keep a close watch over their children and jump into action whenever a problem arises. This can be quite tedious and make it hard to get anything done outside of direct parenting issues. Thus, the lawnmower technique of parenting attempts to create a problem-free environment from the beginning and eliminate the necessity to intervene whenever problems arise. Dan Lacich, my life ling mentor, used this analogy to illustrate that God is not a lawnmower parent. He has not put us in a problem-free environment but has done quite the opposite. He has put us in a situation in which we can not survive without him.

Most parents think that the first thing children need is love and care and that the second thing they need is discipline and boundaries. However, Hebrews 12: 5-11 illustrates that to love a child means to raise it in discipline, and not to raise a child in discipline equates with not living the child.

> "And have you completely forgotten this word of encouragement that addresses you as a father addresses his son? It says, "My son, do not make light of the Lord's discipline, and do not lose heart when he rebukes you, because the Lord disciplines the one he loves, and he chastens everyone he accepts as his son." Endure hardship as discipline; God is treating you as his children. For what children are not disciplined by their father? If you are not disciplined—and everyone undergoes discipline—then you are not legitimate, not true sons and daughters at all. Moreover, we have all had human fathers who disciplined us and we respected them for it. How much more should we submit to the Father of spirits and live! They disciplined us for a little while as they thought best; but God disciplines us for our good, so that we may share in his holiness. No discipline seems pleasant at the time, but painful. Later on, however, it produces a harvest of righteousness and peace for those who have been trained by it" (Hebrews 12: 5-11).

With that in mind, let us take a look at how God has raised his children. But first, it is necessary to clarify whom I am speaking of when I refer to God's Children. Literally, we are all God's Children, but for the purpose of this model of character development, I am referring to the people of Israel figuratively as a single child for the sake of simplicity. The story of Israel's birth began in Gen. 12:2 when God told Abraham that he would be the father of a great nation. Abraham is born a son, Isaac, who is born a son, Jacob, who is later renamed Israel. Israel is then born 12 sons, who then become the 12 tribes of Israel. Thus, the story of God's children begins with Israel's birth, consisting of 12 tribes/families. Figuratively speaking, in its infancy, the newborn nation of Israel was very well cared for in the cradle of Egypt under Joseph, the 11th son of Jacob (aka Israel).

The Infant Stage 0-2 years – Abraham to Joseph

In its infancy, which could be considered the time between Abraham and Joseph, Israel had all of its problems taken care of without taking on any responsibilities of its own. Mistakes were made as often as a baby dirties its diaper. Still, God merely changed the diaper, put the baby in a new diaper, put some soothing baby powder on it, gave it a fresh bottle of warm milk, and laid it in a warm crib to rest and look up at a heavenly mobile. In this stage, there were no harsh punishments, no punishments at all. Like a newborn Baby, Israel, at this point, had no responsibilities to fulfill. Like a newborn baby, food was given right into its mouth, and the kaka simply wiped away.

Some examples of such dirty diapers would be Abraham lying that his wife was his sister so that people would treat him better. He did this twice with no consequence to him. Isaac treated his sons and wives unfairly but without any consequence to himself. Jacob lied to his father and cheated his brother without consequence. Later, Jacob treated his sons unfairly, who, in turn, sold one of their brothers into slavery and lied to their father about it. Again and again, the baby Israel made a mess, and God simply cleaned it up and made it all better, without the baby Israel having to put forth any effort at all.

This is exactly how we treat our babies. They cry out, we come and fix the problem, night and day, day for day, without requiring the baby to put forth any effort of its own. No matter the problem, we as parents simply fix it and cater to the baby's every need and want. That is, as long as it is a baby. After about two years of this, the toddler stage is reached, and then we are not so enthusiastic about catering to the child's every single need and want, day and night.

The difference between a child and an adult is responsibility. Babies have absolutely no responsibilities at all. Food and drink are put in their mouths, their butts wiped, and for their every need attended. However, as a child grows older, they are expected to take on more and more responsibilities. That is why an adult, who does not take on the responsibilities that one would expect from an adult, may be described as childish. Indeed, learning to take on responsibilities, i.e., growing up, is hard. But we all have to do it, one way or another.

The Toddler Stage 2-5 years – Moses to Joshua

The story from Moses to Joshua corresponds with the toddler stage of development (2-5 years), in which Israel learned what happens to one who does not follow God's laws. In this development stage, the people of Israel acted as if there were in their terrible twos. As soon as their preschool teacher Moses turned his back, they were getting into trouble. They were continually whining and complaining, and God had to smack their asses from time to time. Can anyone relate? This was when God set down the Law and did not budge from it a bit. This is absolutely necessary at this stage of development. If a child can do whatever they want at this stage of development, then the parents will be spending the rest of the developmental stages trying to regain the control that they have lost.

Models of Development

And so, the nation of Israel, who at first had its every need fulfilled, in its infancy, later had to learn that life is not so easy. The book of Exodus begins with the people of Israel, who had become more and mightier than the Egyptians, was made to labor rigorously (Ex. 1: 8-14). It may seem extreme to compare the requirements one may pose on a two-year-old to slave labor. But for a small being, whose consciousness consists only of the experience that as soon as a need or desire arose, someone came and fulfilled their needs and desires; any requirement at all may feel like slave labor to them. And often, they will react as such.

From about the age of two, commonly known as the terrible twos, parents may not think it is so cute anymore when they throw their food across the dining room table and giggle in delight at the sound of food splattering on the floor, or when they refuse to eat, sleep, drink, stop crying, etc. There comes a time when even a small child is given some expectations. When this happens, conflict is inevitable. However, problems arise and tend to worsen when a parent is so used to catering to the child's every need that the parent has difficulties requiring a child to take on any responsibilities at all. And so, the toddler begins to raise the parent. I remember reading in one of my child development textbooks that small children, even without the capability of speech, are skilled in communicating their needs. I laughed out loud when I read that and thought, this psychologist obviously does not have a child of their own. Toddlers have no idea what they need; all they know is what they want, and yes, they are extremely skilled in expressing and receiving what they want. So much so that the nurturing parent may confuse what the toddler wants with what the toddler needs. If this happens, a course may be set that becomes very difficult to correct the longer it is held.

God never confuses what his children want with what they need. And although he sympathizes with our pain and suffering, if he knows that situation will give us an opportunity to grow, He will subject us to such trials and tribulations. Und while the slavery to which the Israelites were subjected is, of course, an extreme contrast, in relation to what I have experienced in my work with parents of children with behavioral problems, it is a contrast from which one could gain significant insight towards the importance of discipline in the toddler stage of development.

So if we equate Israel's subjection to slavery with today's parents' introduction to rules, boundaries, and discipline in the lives of our children, we can compare Israel's reaction to that of our toddlers today. Anyone who has kids will have experienced something like this at some point. For about the first two years, adults dress their children and put shoes on them. At first, it is kind of like putting a squirming worm on a limp, flimsy, and floppy hook. But after a while, the child and the parent become a team, and the act of getting dressed gets easier until the child can essentially put their shoes on by themselves. Until one day, when the parent is pressed for time and tells the child, "put your shoes on." We know the child can do it, but suddenly it seems the child cannot. Usually, it is the case that the child simply does not want to do it. Then, almost out of nowhere, a temper tantrum ensues.

And this is where parents tend to make the mistake of reacting to the crying rather than reacting to the situation. The situation is this: The parent told the child to put on their shoes and, for whatever reason, refused to comply although the child is capable of putting their shoes on. Instead, the child throws a fit, screams, cries, and tantrums. If it were possible to translate these behaviors into comprehensible verbal communications, what do you think they would express. Probably some like, "damn it, NO! I am not putting my shoes on, I'm not going anywhere, I want to play with my ... and you can't make me do anything else. And if you try, I'm going to throw such a fit, the neighbors are going to think that you are abusing me!!! So, bring it on!!!"

So, ask yourself. If a two-year-old could verbally express itself in a manner such as that, would you react any differently than you would if the child expressed itself in only a nonverbal tantrum? One might expect that most parents would react to these two communications quite differently. For this reason, it is extremely important to react to the situation rather than to the child's crying; and, this is exactly what God does throughout the Exodus.

Exodus begins by stating that Israel is actually more powerful than Egypt (Ex.1:9-10). Thus, the Egyptians fear that if anyone attacks them, then the Israelites might join forces against them, and Egypt would have no chance. So, Egypt enslaves Israel and does everything to keep them in their place. Does this sound familiar? Has your child ever been bullied by someone? Most parents know that if they step in right away, their child will never learn to fend for themselves, and so we first tend to coach the child through the situation and see how the child reacts instinctively. Some toddlers rise to the occasion and defend themselves, while others fold under pressure. In such situations, the parents keep a close eye on the situation, but depending on the course of the events, the parents may step in sooner or later and balance out their toddler's struggle.

With that in mind, let us study the situation with the toddler Israel in a sandbox with the more worldly mature, but not physically stronger Egypt. At first, the two are playing quite nicely together, but then Egypt begins to notice that Israel's sandcastles are better than their own. Egypt does not want that and begins to take charge of the sandbox. Israel's Father keeps a close eye on the situation, but knowing that Israel is capable of handling the situation by himself, He does not rush in and take immediate control of the situation. He waits to see what his child does.

So, what does Israel do? He takes the easy way out and lets the bully take control of the sandbox. That is what usually happens, and there is no real shame in that. After being confronted with many bullies in their lives, adults know that bullies do not stop until someone fights back. And then they generally look for an easier victim after that, who does not fight back. That is a sad fact of life, but a fact of life that everyone needs to learn, and the first lesson is often taught/fought in the sandbox.

So, even though Israel is stronger, they let themselves be enslaved by Egypt while God the Father watches on, to see how they deal with this bully. And then it happened that Israel reached the point and began to stand up to Egypt, the bully, secretly only appearing to comply with the bully's demands (Ex. 1:15-22). Now imagine your child is playing in the sandbox with another child, and you see the child taking away the toys of your child and smashing the sandcastle of your child. At what point do you get involved. I would expect that most parents would begin to intervene when their child makes a failed effort to resist the bully. When this happens, we might coach from the sidelines and say something like, "that's it, tell 'em that's your shovel and play on that side." And then we sit and watch closely again, monitoring the situation.

Through Israel's secret defiance of Pharaoh, Moses is born, who eventually stands up to the bully, destroys the bully's sandcastles, takes away the bully's toys, and leaves the bully crying alone in the sandbox. In one sentence, this sums up the story of Moses freeing Israel from slavery in Egypt. However, it did not go as smoothly as that. Egypt certainly resisted Israel's freedom, as one would have expected, but Israel resisted their freedom as well. Even Moses felt inadequate to lead Israel away from Egypt, and on several occasions, Israel fought Moses and resisted being freed.

So let us return to our sandbox analogy. Imagine your child is playing in a sandbox with a bully. You see your child attempting to resist the bully but struggling to do so. You see your child's internal conflict. He wants to fight back but is scared to do so. And the initial backlash of the bully from your child's resistance stresses your child out so much that you have to say enough is enough, and so you step in the sandbox yourself.

So, yes, God allowed Israel to be cast into slavery because Israel was physically strong enough to fight back. Still, being only a toddler at this point, Israel was not emotionally or mentally strong enough to overcome the stress associated with fighting off a bully. So, to reinforce Israel's bully resisting behavior, God stepped in at just the right time and empowered Israel to take action. And because God has the power, and because He had a point to make to both his child and the bully. He wanted to teach his child some things about how to deal with stress, how to fight back, and when. But the main lesson he wanted to teach His toddler Israel is that "I AM your Father, and no one messes with your Father."

This reminds me of a wrestling match I once had. I was on the mat and did not even notice any of this at the time, but I did notice that my match had somehow become the main focus of the entire gymnasium, which was strange because it was an early-round in the tournament. Apparently, the coach or the father of my opponent or someone rooting for my opponent said something that was unpleasing to my father. I do not think I have mentioned this yet, but my father is Jon Kolb, former offensive tackle for the Pittsburgh Steelers and at the time one of the strongest men in the world, 6' 2", 240 lbs. And not that it would have been necessary, but his friend Terry Long also from the same caliber and offensive lineman for the Pittsburgh Steelers, was with him. The two of them stood up and walked over to the opposing side, which is all it took to silence the obscenities. Like I said, I was on the mat wrestling at the time and had only heard of the situation after the match. But upon hearing what had happened, not only did I know my father was not going to let anything happen to be, but so did everyone else in the gymnasium.

So, over the course of events told in Exodus chapters 4 to 14, God leads his children out of slavery with such a display of power that one would have thought that the toddler Israel would know that their heavenly Father would never allow anyone or anything to harm them. But such are toddlers, whose compliance in any one situation is not readily transferred to the following situations. Thus, again and again, the toddler Israel lashed out in temper tantrums whenever something did not go the want they wanted or expected. Through various miraculous acts, God saved them. But then the water ran out, and the toddler threw a fit. So, God provided water through a miracle. But then that water ran out, and again Israel threw another fit. God provided water again through another miracle. Then the food ran out, which led to another temper tantrum, so God provided food through another miracle. Then Israel got sick of eating that food and had another hissy fit. God provided, miraculously, another source of food. And it was not as if God only appeared when a problem arrived. No, He made his presents visibly known though a pillar of white smoke during the day and a pillar of fire at night. Still, the toddler fussed and complained during the whole trip to the promised land, "are we there yet, are we there yet, how much longer..." Eventually, any parent will say enough is enough, stop the car and punish the toddler for his continual and unjustified whining.

Today, there are a lot of opinions on the topic of punishment. And this topic will be addressed later in greater detail. Thus, for now, I will only point out that scientific psychology has found that if inappropriate behavior is allowed to continue without punishment, it will become understood as acceptable behavior. Thus, at some point, rules and regulations need to be laid out and clarified. And once this is done, if punishment does not follow when the rules are broken, then the rules are rendered null and void. Furthermore, if existing rules have been rendered null and void, then any additional rules that may follow will not be accepted from the very beginning.

Thus, God clamps down on the Toddler Israel, who simply had to be made to follow the rules. This is again, where many would argue that the God of Israel, who claims to be a loving and just God, is not at all loving or just. After Israel is brought out of slavery and continues to bitch and moan and break the rules, God's wrath falls upon the insubordinate so that only two of them, and by now they number in the thousands, are allowed to enter the promised land. Even Moses, who gets so frustrated with the Toddlers that He disobeys a direct commandment from God, is not allowed to enter the Promised land. Only Caleb and Joshua come to realize that the only way to avoid punishment is to do exactly what God commands, without any backtalk.

And so, under the leadership of Caleb and Joshua, Israel develops from the toddler stage to the stage of childhood.

The Childhood stage 5-12 years – Joshua to David

As previously stated, Kohlberg's model of moral development suggested that toddlers comply with rules to avoid punishment, while children comply with rules to receive rewards. Similarly, while the Exodus story illustrates what happens when one does not obey God, the story of Joshua to David maintains a high standard of obedience but also illustrates the blessings one can experience through good obedience. After 40 years of wandering through the desert, in the continual visual presents of God, Israel reached the land that God promised to give them, only to find that it was inhabited by a mighty nation. And so, after experiencing all the wonders miracles that God performed for them to provide for their needs and keep them safe from their enemies, Israel once again threw a temper tantrum and even said that it would have been better for them to have remained slaves in Egypt, or have simply died in the desert. Only Caleb and Joshua said, 'Let's do this!'

God was, of course, quite put out, to say the least. So He sent them all back into the desert for another forty years, until this disobedient and ungrateful generation died off, and a new generation under Joshua's leadership was raised. After these forty years, this generation was ready to take the land. They were not physically any different. They were not given any superpowers. The only difference was their trust in the Lord, their thankfulness for the gift they were about to receive, and their obedience.

The story of how the Israelites took the city of Jericho illustrates their faithfulness because what God told them to do, which they carried out to the T, was a bit... dare I say ridiculous. They were told to march around the city in perfect silence once a day for six days, and then on the seventh day, they were to march around the city seven times. Then, upon completing the seven rounds, they were all to scream and yell when Joshua blew his horn. I have heard many sermons on this story, and most suggested that God's purpose in doing so was to confuse and scare the enemy, which I am sure it did. But I think what God wanted to do is to make sure Israel was willing to be completely obedient and do what it is told without any complaining or backtalk. Sure, some of the soldiers asked Joshua if he perhaps misunderstood the commands, for let us face it, the idea does seem a bit ridiculous. Nevertheless, the Israelites followed every single command, and as they yelled and Joshua blew his horn, the city walls fell, and the city was theirs. What followed was a series of attacks on various well-fortified cities, but the Israelites essentially ran them all down, except for one small set back.

God had told the Israelites not to take any of the plunder from the victory, but one man, Achan, did just that. And so God stopped their progress until Achan stepped forward and admitted what he had done (Joshua 7 & 8). After that, it was pretty smooth sailing, and the Israelites took the land that God promised them and still have it today.

The book of Judges follows, with which the story of Samson also illustrates that one receives rewards for doing what God commands and punishment for not doing what He commands. God did not ask much of Samson, only that he never ever cut his hair. Sampson was a bit childish. He wanted what he wanted, and with his God-given super strength, he more or less just took what he wanted; and, his enemies could do nothing about it. But in the end, he wanted a woman who was simply and obviously not trustworthy. She finally got him to do the one thing God told him not to do. And so, because of his disobedience, he lost His gift of super strength that God had given him and was captured.

But as if God were introducing a higher stage of childhood, God allowed Sampson to redeem Himself. The simple fact of the matter is: it is impossible to be 100% obedient 100% of the time. Man is simply sinful and disobedient to God. As such, children, even the most well-behaved, will, at times, be disobedient. But I can tell you nothing warms my heart as much as when my children come to me and tell me what

Models of Development

they did wrong and say they are sorry before I even know that they did something wrong. People who know me will attest to the fact that I am very consequent with my children. I do not allow them to talk back, be disrespectful or disobedient to me at all. For such infractions, a consequence (a kinder word for punishment, but punishment all the same) follows immediately. However, if they point them out themselves and offer redemption, then they know that they have no harsh punishment to fear, or at least a much milder one than if they had not come to me. Thinking back now, I cannot even remember the last time my 8-year-old received a harsh punishment, but I can remember dozens of times I swelled with pride as she told me that she felt sorry because she was not nice to another child in school or because she admitted to telling a white lie.

The willingness or desire to make amends and redeem oneself is a character attribute that can begin and should begin to develop in childhood. Furthermore, it may be argued that this is a character attribute that can not be taught directly but only learned through the experience of loving discipline as described in Hebrews chapter 12. So if Joshua is an example of early childhood, where the child does what is asked of him, more or less blindly, to receive rewards, Sampson may be an example of mid-childhood, where the child usually does what is asked of him, but also expresses the desire to redeem himself when he fails to be obedient. Examples of late childhood characteristics may be found in the story about King Saul and King David.

Saul was the first King of Israel. And initially, he did a good job of following the Lord and leading Israel. That is until he showed initiative. This is a story of the Bible that I had a hard time understanding until I had children of my own. Saul did something here that made him lose favor with God forever. It must be something really bad, right? Something like Idol worship, adultery, murder? No, Saul only offered a burnt offering to the Lord, but He was told not to do that until Samuel arrived. However, the enemy was closing in and about to attack. With the enemy closing in and Samuel, who was supposed to make the offering, was nowhere to be found, Saul took it upon himself to make the offering. He knew He was not supposed to do this, but he certainly did not want to have to go into battle without first giving an offering. From Saul's perspective, his decision to go ahead and make the offering himself does make sense. He simply chose what he thought was the lesser of two wrongs. But Saul's perspective is not the perspective that counts. Who, what, and how offerings are made are of the utmost importance. Essentially, that is the general message of the Gospel: Jesus said I am the way the truth and the life; no one comes to the Father except through me.

Saul was well on his way to becoming a great king. He had the King thing down pretty well, but he overstepped his bounds and thought he knew better and took the matter into his own hands. Older children, especially if they are good, well-behaved, and obedient children, can make this mistake as well. If they are raised well, they take on responsibility and do what is asked of them. If they do it well and are rewarded, this builds confidence, which of course, is a good thing. However, as confidence builds, it tends to swell and become overconfident, which is not so good. But professionally speaking, as a psychologist, too much confidence is better than too little confidence. So, please do not read this and think you automatically need to put your older child back in his place. Nevertheless, Saul's story points out that older children may need a healthy setback from time to time after enjoying some significant success. Otherwise, they may begin to believe they know better than they actually do.

Granted, today, parents generally do not punish cases of overconfident disobedience so severely, but in Saul's case, his disobedience was followed by great and everlasting bitterness. But as I pointed out earlier, God's punishment today comes in the form of natural consequences. I am reluctant to offer any such examples of my children's overconfident disobedience. But upon asking my father if he recalled any such examples, he has called me three times this morning with more examples of overconfident disobedience of part of his children. The simple fact of the matter is, the better we get at something, the better we think we are at it, but we are never as good at it as we think. This is especially true when it comes to following God.

After Saul came David, David too overstepped his bounds, later in life, but he differed with Saul in how he reacted to the setbacks of failures due to overconfidence. Where Saul grew more and more spiteful, David grew more and more humble. David was eager to grow and learn. He was obedient, but he also crossed the line from time to time. But when he did, he did not express spite or resentment; instead, he expressed humility and repentance. How did David learn this, and how can we teach this to our children? Honestly, I am not sure that is possible. After we have taught our children right from wrong, by consequently punishing the wrong and rewarding the right, there comes the point in which our words and actions as parents become an insignificant influence, and we lose the authority we once had. Even if we feel as if our child is not ready to take on the challenges of the adult world by themselves, in the end, it is not our decision. Sure, in some cases, it is the parent who kicks the child out of the nest, but in most cases, it is the child who claims to be ready and grown up against the parent's recommendations. But, when it comes to this point, that is all the parent can do, make recommendations. From this point on, it is no longer the parent, who decides what the child is to learn, but rather it is the child who gets to decides what he or she wants to learn.

The difficult thing for a child to learn in this stage of character development is that even if others do not follow the rules, it is still better to do. That is a hard lesson to learn, but eventually, one can learn that being spiteful just makes things worse. But if we learn to be patient, even the most difficult problems can be solved. Having now learned to follow the rules, we are presented with something new: responsibility and the pros and cons that come with it. It is also at this age that relationships with peers begin to develop. It is no longer the case that we are only cared for, but we begin to care about others as well.

Saul was king, but he blew it. David was to follow, and so Saul did all he could to kill him, run him off, or in any way get rid of David. Still, David did not return hate with hate. Instead, he respected Saul, as king anointed by God, and waited patiently. David knew he was next in line. Everyone knew it, even Saul. That is why Saul hated him so much. Still, David concentrated on following God, learning patiently, and developing into the person God gave him the potential to become. He still made mistakes. In fact, one could easily argue that he made more and greater mistakes than Saul did, but David learned from his mistakes. He improved himself and grew with the challenges of this world.

Adolescence (12-18) – Psalms, Proverbs, Job, and the Prophets

After David's story, the rest of the Bible begins to jump around a lot more and not follow a chronological order. The Psalms and Proverbs are not written in a story format but resemble much more a literature textbook. The story of Job is indeed a story but goes beyond telling what happens and ventures into the discussion of why it happens. The prophets could be described as written in a short story format but require a comprehensive analysis to get the whole story. As such, this next section of the Bible takes us to school as we learn to analyze the literature and philosophy that describes what it means to walk with God.

After grade school comes high school. The two differ in the curriculum and intensity, which increases exponentially in the undergraduate to graduate levels of education. At this stage, children are expected to study for many hours each day and learn a vast amount of information. Thus, by the time an individual has reached this stage of life, one may expect an individual to act like an adult, or at least to possess the capability to do so upon request for short periods. This seems to be an implication that many junior and high school teachers make when they attempt to call their classes to order with the redundant words, "People can we act like adults now?!?!"

School is perhaps the most significant event in an adolescent stage of life. With that, I do not mean the social aspects of school, but rather the gaining of knowledge on various subjects. Very few embrace this aspect of school, and if they do, they are commonly referred to as nerds. However, it is commonly known, and various movies and stories will attest to this: The high school nerds are often the people who tend to reach higher heights. As such, God also requires his children to learn the Holy scriptures and do so with significant diligence. In the Jewish tradition, learning the scriptures and even the language in which there were originally written, Hebrew, is a central part of their adolescence.

I am sure many a child, living in this Jewish tradition in modern times has exclaimed, "Why do I have to learn this? This has no relevance in my future life." Adolescences complain about having to learn things that they do not need all of the time. And it is nearly impossible to explain to them why they need to learn trigonometry, chemistry, literature, a foreign language, Social Studies, etc. I would argue that if an adolescent were able to understand why they needed to learn these 'pointless' things at this time, they would not be asking the question in the first place. Thus, seldom is an attempt made to explain why we force adolescents to learn various subjects at this stage of their life that they perhaps will never need to know or use again.

But let me venture an explanation. For if God required his children to learn intensely, then there has to be a reason behind it. And there is. And it is quite a simple one. The human brain continues to develop until about the age of 21. Thus, even if a child at the age of 12 can adequately read, write and do arithmetic, his brain is continuing to develop, and to foster this development, it is necessary to have the brain work out. Thus, the history, chemistry, literature, and all of the seemingly pointless subjects that one learns at this stage of development are not because we need this information, but because we need the intense brain exercises at this time of our development. If we do not get these brain workouts at this stage of development, our brain will cease to develop, which will make learning and understanding and overall brain functioning in later stages in life significantly less efficient.

So, when we compare this idea to our spiritual lives, we may find that we have the same sort of thinking as a teenager complaining about geometry. Some of the bible stories that have come up thus far are quite well known by most people regardless of religion or spirituality. But the Psalms, Proverbs, Job, and the Prophets that make up the remainder of the old testament tend to be much less well known and rarely studied. A verse will pop up from psalms or proverbs pasted on a pretty picture in one's Facebook feed. We know Job had it hard, remained faithful to God, and things got better. And we know that the Prophets said a lot of things that have already come true, and the rest will also come true. But many fail to study this material intensely.

I used to teach the Bible story at my church's youth group. But after completing the story of King David, the youth pastor wanted to jump to the new testament, arguing that after David, Israel loses favor with God, then regains favor and then loses it and regains it back and forth until Jesus comes on the scene. While that is more or less true, this back and forth of finding favor and losing favor with God back and forth on a seemingly endless oscillation is an accurate description of what life is like.

However, while knowledge of Moses, the burning bush, the ten commandments, Joseph and the Technicolor coat, Joshua and his Horn and, Sampson and Delilah, and David and Goliath is more than most people know about the Bible and certainly, more than enough to get the gist of the old testament, to merely know this material is not enough. One has to actively study the Bible and search it for answers in your life. Avoid the mentality of the "cool kids" in high school. They thought they did not need to know this stuff. It was not important in the real world, blah blah blah. The excuses are innumerable.

But it is important, extremely important, for life essentially consists of falling on and off of God's path. It is a struggle that we know only when we look back on it. How many times have we stepped on and off of God's path in our lives? More often than we would like to admit and most often for incredibly stupid reasons. The reason that this happens so often is that, at the moment, when we step off of God's path, we do not recognize that we are doing it. It is like this, imagine you are going somewhere, and you are fairly sure you know the way, so you are driving along have a good time, rocking out to you is 'road trip' music. Suddenly, you realize that you are lost: past tense. Nobody realizes that they are getting lost: the present continues. The realization only hits us after it has already happened. Most of the time, no amount of reflection will enable us to remember the exact point where we made the wrong turn. Unless, of course, we know the roads very well. We can sometimes immediately know when we missed a turn, but still only after it has happened. While the popular Bible stories are like the main highways of the map of life, the Psalms, Proverbs, Job, the Prophets, and the rest of the old testament are comparable to the map's back roads of life. They tell us about incidental aspects of life that take much more time to grasp and require a greater amount of cogitation to understand. In this stage of our lives, we expand our reflection of the benefits and consequences of following God's Law and what it means to do so, which is commonly referred to and described as 'Walking with God.' The image that is often associated with the concept of walking with God is the popular poem:

Footprints in the Sand.

One night I dreamed a dream. As I was walking along the beach with my Lord. Across the dark sky flashed scenes from my life. For each scene, I noticed two sets of footprints in the sand, One belonging to me and one to my Lord. After the last scene of my life flashed before me, I looked back at the footprints in the sand. I noticed that at many times along the path of my life, especially at the very lowest and saddest times, there was only one set of footprints.

This troubled me, so I asked the Lord about it. "Lord, you said once I decided to follow you, You'd walk with me all the way. But I noticed that during the saddest and most troublesome times of my life, there was only one set of footprints. I don't understand why, when I needed You the most, You would leave me."

He whispered, "My precious child, I love you and will never leave you Never, ever, during your trials and testings. When you saw only one set of footprints, It was then that I carried you."

While this poem is beautiful, inspiring, and simply lovely, one will still continually stumble upon the situations in which one questions the underlining messages of this image and the various basic Bible stories. Because let us face it: Life is deadly. Life will literally kill us all, and no amount of warm fuzzy thoughts will change that. Life is hard, unfair, and painful at the very least. For some, it is even worse. Others may add pointless, hopeless, and meaningless. But with a deeper understanding of the Holy Scriptures coupled with a significant amount of time of walking with God, one may come to recognize that death lasts a lifetime and only ends upon its inception.

Such thoughts are indicative of this stage of character development, in which we begin to ponder the mysteries of nature and our existence and do so in a more scholastic and abstract manner. This is the period in which we learn that life is not always fair, and sometimes bad things happen even if we are good; and, good things sometimes happen even if we are bad. Sometimes we lash out, sometimes we rejoice, and sometimes it does not even seem to make a difference what we do, think, and say.

It is at this stage of our character development that to continue our development, we need to learn and understand and recognize that,

> "There is a time for everything, and a season for every activity under the heavens: a time to be born and a time to die, a time to plant and a time to uproot, a time to kill and a time to heal, a time to tear down and a time to build, a time to weep and a time to laugh, a time to mourn and a time to dance, a time to scatter stones and a time to gather them, a time to embrace and a time to refrain from embracing, a time t search and a time to give up, a time to keep and a time to throw away, a time to tear and a time to mend, a time to be silent and a time to speak, a time to love and a time to hate, a time for war and a time for peace" (Ecclesiastes 3: 1-8).

These are very hard and deep lessons to learn. But such is life. Yes, we have a God who gives us guidance, but it is still so damn hard to follow. This is a very changing and demanding stage of life, but we will know that we have completed it when, after all of this studying, we eventually come to understand that we really do not know much at all, but we continue to strive to grow none the less. And so, if you have not already done so, go back to the end of the Old Testament, and finish your education. Learn the Psalms and Proverbs and hide them in your heart. Gain a deeper understanding of what was going on between Job and God. Learn the Prophets and realize that prophecy is being fulfilled in our lifetime, right now. For without this knowledge and the experience of gaining this knowledge, you may find that your spiritual capabilities and growth may be lacking something.

Young Adult (18-25) – The Gospels

In this stage of life, the Gospels illustrate the next level of character development. In the last stage, an individual will have expanded their knowledge and understanding and conclude that they do not know all there is to know, but nevertheless understand that there is a truth to be known. The Gospels introduce that truth and illustrate that without God, not only will our knowledge be incomplete, but also our heart, body, mind, and soul will also be incomplete. Moreover, the Gospels explain how one can gain this truth, come to God, and become complete.

The character development at this level requires one to be submissive to God, recognize and admit that one is incomplete, incapable, and inadequate to make it through this world on their own. There comes a day in this stage of character development in which an individual will either decide that they know what is best for their lives and take control, or they will surrender the control of their lives to God. However, what may still be lacking in this stage of character development is the understanding that the decision to give God the control is not a one-time decision, as the decision to invite the Holy Spirit into your heart and accept Jesus's death on the cross as payment for your sins. Do that one time, and you are saved for all eternity. But the decision to give God complete control of your life is a decision that one must make every moment of every day because we humans so often tend to grab the steering wheel and want to take back control from time to time, at least momentarily.

As such, this stage of life can be very distressing. On one side, one will learn Jesus is the way, the truth, and the life. Of that, we are sure. We understand the concept of salvation, the penalty of sin, and why Jesus had to be sentenced to death. We may even begin to gain an understanding of deep theological concepts like predestination, the deity of Christ, the Trinity, and other such questions that theological scholars like to debate and discuss. So, on one side, we feel confident in our understanding, although this understanding includes the fact that we do not, will not, and cannot understand everything. But on the other side, none of this knowledge and understanding makes life any easier. And when trials and tribulations arise, it is so easy to fall into the precarious question, 'Why?'. While the statement, 'God works in mysterious ways' is indeed a profound truth, it is often an unsatisfying answer to questions like, why does my child have cancer? Why did my spouse leave me? Why? Why? Why? In the midst of all the possible why questions, it is easy to reject the possibility that God can and will offer a satisfying answer to all of our' why questions'.

When people get hung up on 'why questions,' they often begin to think and feel that their Spirit is too weak to survive in this world. They feel great sorrow. They feel inadequate. They hunger and thirst for the truth behind all of the 'why questions' that lay outside their reach. And if they dwell too long in these thoughts and feelings, they may very well forget that these thoughts and feelings are the first four Beatitudes. God knows that this world is hard. And while one could discuss the question 'why is it so hard?' No answer, regardless of how satisfying the answer is, will change the fact that life is hard.

Hence the beatitudes exclaim that when we have tried and failed, again and again, when we are lost and have nowhere to go when we feel like giving up and dying. That is the point, right there at the bottom of the murky pit of our disastrous lives, where we are reading and willing to say, "Ok, God, I have tried everything I could think of, I cannot take it anymore. I give up" When we reach that point, then we can begin to understand that it is because of our weakness that we can become strong if we surrender the control of our lives to God (Psalm 73:26; 2. Cor. 12:9-10; Isaiah 40:29; Matt. 11:28; 1. Peter 5:7; Rom. 8:26; Phil. 4:13). But coming to this conclusion, only for a moment, just to reassume control in the next moment, is not how this is meant to work. The Beatitudes are essentially a model of development in and of themselves, in which each level of surrender brings one to the next level of surrender. They continue with attributes of mercy, pureness, and peacefulness. After having reached and obtained all of these attributes, the beatitudes conclude by declaring that not even deliberate persecution will be able to stop, hinder, and deter someone who is empowered by the Holy Spirit of the Living God.

All of this is a big huge chunk of the lesson of life and is a lesson that one may begin to learn in early adulthood, but most likely not completed until much later in life, if at all in many cases. Thus, I would suggest that the latter attributes of this level of character development occur much later in this stage or the next. For, first things first and first, an individual must decide who is in charge of their life. Are they going to maintain control, or are they going to give it to God? If they decide to maintain control themselves, their character development stops where it is. If they decide to give God the control, their character development will continue if they do not continue to grab the steering wheel every time life happens.

Many people come to know, accept, and follow Jesus at a very young age. I did, and so did my children. And although I believe a very young person can sincerely make the decision to follow Jesus and understand what that means, I maintain that it is not until a person reaches adulthood that he or she can truly understand what it means to deny oneself and follow Him. In Matthew 16:24-25 (NIV), "... Jesus said to his disciples, 'Whoever wants to be my disciple must deny themselves and take up their cross and follow me. For whoever wants to save their life will lose it, but whoever loses their life for me will find it.'" It was not until I entered adulthood that I understood that this is not to be taken figuratively but literally.

God made it very easy for me to come to this understanding. Most people are not so fortunate and have to learn this the hard way. The greatest gift God ever gave to me was death. When I was diagnosed with MD, the doctor told me that I had two years to live. After the initial shock that lasted about a week, I decided that I would follow God completely and obediently from that point on. While this is an extremely hard thing to do over the course of an entire life, when one knows that one only has two years to live, it makes it much easier.

And so I became very receptive and obedient to the Spirit of God, not only for the big decisions in my life but in every single decision. For me, in that situation, it was not difficult for me to not worry about tomorrow because I literally did not have one, or at least I thought so at the time. During the week, I worked as a clinic clown, and on the weekends, I did other shows. I just lived day for day, traveling from town to town, doing street performing shows, and talking to people. These talks always turned into talks about God, and I shared my faith and lived like there was no tomorrow, day for day, every day. It was the best time of my life because it seemed like the Kingdom of God was so near.

Eventually, I realized that either God healed me to some extent, in that the MD did not affect the involuntary muscles of my heart, or the doctors diagnosed me wrong. (When MD affects the heart muscle, as is the case in some MD forms, death is imminent. But when MD only affects the skeletal muscles, one can live for quite some time and deteriorate slowly). Either way, I am obviously still alive. But, having already, not only figuratively but literally, denied myself, died, and given this broken life to God, I have gained a new life, one absolutely and completely without fear of anything I could face in life or death. That, my friends, is what the Gospel is about.

As illustrated in the Gospels of Jesus, the young adult stage of life could be compared to the time in a person's life in which they leave the preverbal nest. By this time, the individual has learned to follow the rules and understand their functions. But, more important than this is the appreciation that following rules is not enough. There is a higher Law above the Law, and that is Jesus. So from here, the young adult can begin to learn more about themself and the world around them in preparation for life. By this time, if one has gone through these stages of character development, the Law will have been planted into one's heart, not only so that one can avoid punishment and gain a reward, but simply because it is the right thing to do. And it was with that knowledge that the disciples dropped what they were doing and followed Him.

The challenge with which we are confronted in this stage of our lives is the question of purpose. God creates with purpose, and he created us; thus, He created each of us with a specific purpose. Those who do not walk with God try to find some purpose in their lives. This may lead to life stress because a square peg simply does not fit in a round hole. But then, how do we know what God's purpose is for our lives? The Gospels point out that God has a purpose for each of us, but unfortunately, there is no index which pairs each person in the world with their purpose. We have to figure that out on our own by being extremely attentive to the Holy Spirit.

For so long, science has been trying to create a perpetual mobile, an object that can maintain motion forever. And science has concluded that this is not possible. But Jesus demonstrated that the opposite is true, for we are all perpetual mobiles. The motion begins before and continues after this world. And the people who have chosen to seek and follow God's purpose for their lives will continue to live after they die.

Furthermore, the Gospel teaches that this perpetual motion will begin in this life and continue into the next. But the power that keeps us in motion and growth must come from God. Every time we reassume control of our lives, for whatever reason, and for however long, we take the momentum out of his power out of our lives and replace it with our own weakness again. It takes a continual conscious effort to maintain the decision to give God control of our lives. Maintaining this state of mind is difficult and takes a lifetime to master. The Gospels explain what it means to 'walk with God.' It is a choice to surrender to Him the control of our lives and to do this daily, even hourly, and from moment to moment. He knows this is difficult to do, and He knows that only a few will choose to follow Him (Matthew 22:14).

Adult Stage 25 and older – Act and Epistles

This stage of character development can only occur if one remains empowered by God's Holy Spirit. Acts and the Epistles illustrate what life can be like when one chooses to follow God consistently. It is in this stage that our walk with God begins to take root. But again, what does it mean to walk with God? It means essentially what it sounds like it would mean. To walk with someone means two people are side by side and moving in the same direction. That is, they share space, direction, and thus also time together. When we choose to walk with God, we submit that he knows the best path for our lives. When forks appear in the road, we let Him decide which way we will go. That is, we run every decision by Him; and, life essentially is comprised of a long series of decisions. And should we at times diverge from his path, His Spirit calls out to us and brings us back to him. And it does so one more time than we diverge. However, choosing to follow God can be stressful. So often, He takes us in a direction in which we flat out do not want to go. We question his judgment. But through our character development, this will happen less and less the longer that one has been walking with God. As God's children, we are not as it seems: adults living in this world on our own. If we submit to his authority, as children submit to their parents, our Heavenly Father will offer us guidance throughout our lives, just as we offer our children guidance throughout their lives. In short, if we choose Him, He will choose us (Mat. 22:14; Col. 3-12-17; Luke 18:7; Deut 7:6; 1.Cor.1:26; Eph. 1:4; James 2:5; 1. Peter 2:10)

He offers his counsel when we ask for it. Some seek His guidance more than others. But having drunk from the living water, which is the Holy Spirit, I can attest confidently that the more often one seeks the guidance of the Holy Spirit, the more capable one is in coping with life stress. Nevertheless, remaining continually without fail on God's path is an impossibility. Due to our sinful nature, we inevitably get sidetracked from time to time. However, even though we have understood the good news of the Gospel, that God's Holy Spirit can empower us and that we can be with Him in Heaven someday, none of this changes the fact that momentarily we are living in a corrupted world. This is commonly referred to as life stress, which comes from merely being alive and staying alive. The stress of one's life can be lethal. And that is something that we all have to deal with, whether we have chosen to follow God or not.

It is in our adult stage in life that we come to the realization that we are still children. We act like we are imprisoned in the world and slaves to our sinful desires, just as the Israelites were slaves in Egypt.

Don't you know that when you offer yourselves to someone as obedient slaves, you are slaves of the one you obey—whether you are slaves to sin, which leads to death, or to obedience, which leads to righteousness?

But thanks be to God that, though you used to be slaves to sin, you have come to obey from your heart the pattern of teaching that has now claimed your allegiance. You have been set free from sin and have become slaves to righteousness (Romans 6:16-18 NIV).

The Israelites at that time chose to lash out against God and instead of following Him. The consequence of this was a severe punishment. In our lives today, it is the natural consequence of our actions that serve as punishment in the form of life stress. A single bad decision can have a lasting impact on the rest of our lives. Knowing this makes it all the more difficult to think clearly and manage one's emotions, thoughts, words, and behaviors. Being stressed out is not a problem. A problem, par definition, is something with a solution; there is no way to avoid stress. The problem arises when we get so stressed out that we lash out against anyone or anything. God, did not command us not to get emotional. He made us emotional. But he did say that we should not let our emotions drive us to sin. Paul explains it this way:

> "Did that which is good, then, become death to me? By no means! Nevertheless, in order that sin might be recognized as sin, it used what is good to bring about my death, so that through the commandment sin might become utterly sinful. We know that the law is spiritual; but I am unspiritual, sold as a slave to sin. I do not understand what I do. For what I want to do I do not do, but what I hate I do. And if I do what I do not want to do, I agree that the law is good. As it is, it is no longer I myself who do it, but it is sin living in me. For I know that good itself does not dwell in me, that is, in my sinful nature. For I have the desire to do what is good, but I cannot carry it out. For I do not do the good I want to do, but the evil I do not want to do—this I keep on doing. Now if I do what I do not want to do, it is no longer I who do it, but it is sin living in me

that does it. So I find this law at work: Although I want to do good, evil is right there with me. For in my inner being I delight in God's law; but I see another law at work in me, waging war against the law of my mind and making me a prisoner of the law of sin at work within me." Romans 7:13-23 NIV

This passage reads as if Paul were on his psychologist's couch, and essentially he is. Indeed God is a wonderful counselor. But I think I have learned from my experiences as a psychological counselor. It does not matter at all how good the counselor is. If the client does not want to change, then no change will take place. It is the client who has to be willing to listen, reflect, work, and eventually change. But too often, as adult children of God, we seem to think that we know what is best for our lives, in the same mentality that our teenage children often think they know better than their parents.

In accordance with the concept of being born again, each of us goes through the above character development twice. Or at least we should go through it twice (John 3:5-8). The first time is during our physical development. We start out as babies and develop into adults, and during this time, we go through the sequential stage as previously discussed. However, as adults, to come to know what God's purpose is for our lives, we need to go through this entire developmental process again, but on a spiritual level. Paul concurs in 1. Cor. 13:11, as he points out, "When I was a child, I talked like a child, I thought like a child, I reasoned like a child. When I became a man, I put the ways of childhood behind me." When we reach the point in our adult lives where we realize that life stress is continually beating down on us, and we reach a point beyond which we simply can not continue to grow. That is, we are saved, we have faith, we do our best to uphold the Law, we read the Bible, go to church, we have a prayer life, we embrace what is good, we do all the things a good Christians and does, and we even understand that it is by God's grace that we are saved, and not because of all the things we do. But still, life happens at times, and we get crushed, again and again. Afterward, we turn back to God, we redeem and restore, and heal, only to get crushed from something later down the path. What can we do to stop from getting crushed?

We need to realize that we were born slaves to this world and to our flesh. We need to realize that we can not break free from this sin on our own. We need to realize that if we follow the Word of God, we will be blessed with the strength to overcome life stress, but not relieved from life stress. We need to realize that we need to study the word of God intensely and keep it in our hearts and minds through meditation and prayer. We need to realize that through Jesus Christ, we can be (and must be) made new every day, so that past failure can no longer bring us down. The Apostle Paul demonstrated that he had come to these realizations, in that he learned that suffering brings perseverance; perseverance brings character; Character brings hope (Romans 5:3). In addition to that, He got so accustomed to being strengthened by the Holy Spirit in the midst of trials and tribulations that he began to greet life stress with the expectation of victory. In fact, he had experienced the power of God in the face of adversity so often that he began to delight and boast of his weaknesses because when life came at him, his guardian angel said, "Hold my beer."

Finally, while Paul was certainly a man who walked with God and he did a wonderful job in his writing, I would like to humbly offer him this one critique: In the Romans 8: 35-39 passage, where he answers the question, "Who shall separate us from the love of Christ?" I think he could have been a little bit clearer if he had answered directly rather than indirectly. He begins by listing a few specific things that can not separate us from the love of Christ: trouble, hardship, persecution, famine, nakedness, danger, or sword. Then he continues listing various spectrum of things that can not separate us from the love of God. But while he seemingly covers all the bases and seems to suggest that nothing can separate us from the love of Christ, He does distinctly leave one thing open. Can you catch it?

For I am convinced that neither death nor life, neither angels nor demons, neither the present nor the future, nor any powers, neither height nor depth, nor anything else in all creation, will be able to separate us from the love of God that is in Christ Jesus our Lord (Romans 8:38-39 NIV).

So what can separate us from the love of God? If you still think the answer is "nothing," then read the passage again. Paul describes that almost nothing can separate us from the Love of God, by illustrating that nothing between the opposite ends of various spectrums can separate us from the Love of God: Death – Life; Angels – Demons, Height – Depth; PRESENT or FUTURE. Do you see it now? Do you see what he specifically left out? The Past! The past can separate us from the love of God if we hang on to it. If we ponder it in our hearts and minds, we live in the past, either because it was so good we do not want to let go of it, or because it was so bad that we cannot let go of it, or for any other reason, then we will have a hard time letting Jesus erase it and make us new.

It is very hard for some, and my heart pours out to them that struggle to let go of the past, of things that hold them away from God. This is especially hard when the wounds are still fresh and bleeding. The only means of healing that I know comes through the decision to not figuratively but literally give your whole life to Christ and follow Him. Then you, too, will experience the awesome power that comes from being filled, empowered, and guided by the Holy Spirit. And while life may knock and shake you a little, nothing will ever crush you again.

Chapter Four

Learning Behaviors

Scientific psychology has found that one may foster childhood development and learning behaviors by applying therapeutic methods. While learning behavior is typically associated with childhood development rather than adulthood, the same concepts apply. It is very well possible to teach an old dog a new trick, but it is certainly a little more difficult. Nevertheless, it is often a necessity that adults, as much as children, learn to change their behaviors. For this purpose, one may choose to seek help from a mental health practitioner.

Very simply put, there are two types of psychotherapy: Behavioral Psychotherapy and Psychoanalysis. These two techniques pursue the same goal, which is change but are based on different principles. Psychoanalysis explores the past in an attempt to change the future, while behavioral therapy tends to focus more on the present. In addition to this, and again I am speaking here very generally, psychoanalysis tends to focus on thoughts, ideas, emotions, personality, attitude, and such complex constructs that may be anchored deep in one's subconscious. In contrast, behavioral therapy tends to be based more on behaviorism. Behaviorism differs from psychology in that it maintains that abstract concepts such as personality, emotion, attitude, etc., are not viable, observable, and measurable concepts. Furthermore, the only thing that is viable, observable, and measurable is behavior. Thus, behaviorism tends to neglect the many various abstract concepts previously listed and focuses on behavior alone. Both techniques have their pros and cons and also tend to be used for different psychological problems.

Applied Behavioral Analysis (ABA) is a therapeutic learning method that is based on basic psychological structures of how all organisms learn, as outlined by Skinner and Pavlov. Most frequently, this method of therapeutic learning has become the most effective teaching method implemented with children with a persuasive developmental disorder such as Autism. However, because ABA is based on the fundamental building blocks of functional learning, it can, and I dare say, should be applied to all aspects of learning and on all stages of development.

As such, ABA has formulated an equation that links behavior to motivation, reinforcement, and consequence. This equation applies to essentially all living organisms. This equation is: Behavior = Motivation + (Reinforcement ÷ Consequence). That is, all living creatures do what they have to do to get what they want if they want it bad enough. This asserts that no behavior is random. We may not consciously know why we perform a specific behavior, but somewhere, at the very least, deep in our sub-consciousness, the reason for any behavior can be found. In order to understand how this equation works, it may be necessary to first define the terms of the equation.

Behavior is defined as any and all bodily movements. This includes skeletal movements, verbal actions, non-verbal communications, and involuntary actions. Whenever a person's body moves in any way, this is what we call behavior. Thus the ultimate goal of behavioral therapy is to help an individual change their behavior. Try as we might, no one has any direct influence on the behavior of any other person, but we can influence it indirectly through motivation, reinforcement, and consequence.

Motivation may be described as the drive behind the behavior. If behavior is what one is doing, then motivation is why they are doing it. For example, have you ever been watching a movie at the theater, and while you were watching, you slowly begin to notice that your bladder is full, and you simply have to relieve yourself. But the movie is just too suspenseful at that moment. What do you do? You hold it and hold it until the motivation to relieve yourself (in the bathroom) exceeds the motivation to watch the movie against the consequence of wetting your pants versus missing a part of the movie. If it is a really great movie and you are totally into it, you will hold out much longer than you would if the movie is not too much to your liking. But let us say it is, and you are at the edge of your seat. At some point, the motivation to go to the bathroom will win because regardless of how good the movie is, the suspense will inevitably fall back a little at some point. When that happens, the motivation of not wetting your pants will exceed the motivation of not missing anything, and you will get up and go.

Reinforcement is simply a fancy term for the things that we want. How bad we want them depends on two things. First, the motivation previously discussed and the costs associated with the reinforcement. If you are familiar with the TV advertisement, "What would you do for a Klondike Bar," then you are already familiar with the concept. The ad asserts that Klondike bars are so good, anyone would do anything to get one, no matter the costs. But what if the reinforcement is good, but not that good? Then the motivation and costs play a more significant role in the behavior required to obtain the reinforcement at that moment.

Let us say you are hiking and you get really, really thirsty, and you come across a pond with algae growing in it. In this situation, water is a strong reinforcement for you. You want it, and you even need it. But would you drink the water out of the scum pond or wait till you found some fresher water? It would depend on how thirsty you are? If you were on the verge of death through dehydration, then this scummy water would be a true blessing. If you are only mildly thirsty, you want water, but do you want this water? The answer lies in your motivation, as previously described, but also in the consequences. The water from the pond would surely relieve your thirst, but could it also make you sick? That would be a consequence that one may consider.

On the other hand, let us say you are walking, but you are not so thirsty. But you know, up on top of a high hill, there is a fresh spring of the best water on the planet. Because of that, you may venture the hill, not because you are so thirsty, but because the water (the reinforcement) is so good.

Reinforcement and consequence are the more complicated elements of this equation that must be defined a bit further to portray their functioning accurately and properly. First of all, the consequence of a behavior can be either good or bad, but most likely a degree of both good and bad at the same time. The good consequence is called reinforcement, and the bad consequence is called a punishment. Therapeutically speaking, a reinforcement is something that is given into a situation when one sees a behavior that one would like to see more frequently. Similarly, a punishment is something that is given into a situation when one sees a behavior that one would like to see less frequently. Consequences for our behaviors do not only occur in structured learning situations, but they also occur naturally in everyday life.

In the previous example, the reinforcement of going to the bathroom is that one no longer has the extremely uncomfortable pressure in the bladder. This is a perfect example of a negative reinforcement. In this case, negative does not mean bad, but rather the subtraction of something bad, while a positive reinforcement is the addition of something good. As such, the consequence of going to the bathroom, despite the motivation to stay and continue watching the movie, is the removal or subtraction of bladder discomfort. When this therapeutic method is used in working with children with behavioral issues, negative reinforcements are not often used because it entails removing a discomfort. That is something we tend to do for children regardless of their behavior. However, I did have a client who had very dry skin and loved to have his back scratched so much that he would even do his math homework for a little back-scratching. Thus, having figured this out, his mom no longer had to fight with him to get him to do his homework but merely sat down next to him and chatted in her handy with one hand and scratched his back with the other, while the child diligently did his math homework.

A positive reinforcement is what one gets out of performing a particular action. In our movie bathroom example, the positive reinforcement of getting up and going to the bathroom is that one then gets to watch the rest of the movie in comfort, which is certainly much more enjoyable. Most potty training techniques implement the use of positive reinforcement. That is, the child is given a reward for timely going to the toilet. However, in some cases, a child may so dislike having a dirty diaper, so the negative reinforcement of not feeling the discomfort of a dirty diaper is sufficient for potty training.

The above were examples of natural consequences. If we do something, good or bad, consequences will follow that will influence how we behave in similar situations in the future. This natural system can thus be used to influence the behavior of our children. When we see them demonstrate good behavior, we can reinforce this behavior, which will increase the likelihood that this type of behavior will be demonstrated more frequently. Or when we see them demonstrate bad behavior, we can punish this behavior, which will decrease the likelihood that this type of behavior will be demonstrated more frequently. But how should we discipline? Scientific psychology has found that there are two kinds of discipline: positive and negative. Again, in this context, positive and negative do not refer to good and bad discipline, but rather positive discipline is when we give something into a situation, and negative discipline is when we take something out of a situation.

Typically, parents tend to resort to negative punishments such as the beloved grounding, followed by no telephone, TV, PlayStation, or whatever the child wants that can be taken away from him. A classic example of positive discipline is illustrated in every introduction to a Simpsons episode where Bart is made to write a statement on the chalkboard many times.

Scientific psychology has found that positive discipline is more effective than negative discipline (Giles, Sneihotta, McColl, & Adams, 2015). The reason for this is that negative discipline is limited and may lead to resentment. That is, we can only take away so much from a child.

And if we take away too much, the child is likely to become resentful, develop the attitude of apathy, and come to the conclusion, 'I now have nothing and can do nothing, so what more can they do to me.' In addition to this, negative discipline is often removed in time significantly from the moment of the inappropriate behavior. For example, a child comes home from school and immediately does something bad, to which the parents declare, "No TV tonight, now go do your homework." This can go wrong in two ways. The child can think, well then there is no need to do my homework now if I already cannot watch TV tonight. Or, the child could do his homework exceptionally well and demonstrate other good behaviors. In this case, one may find it difficult to enforce the TV ban due to the exceptionally good behavior that was demonstrated most recently.

However, with a positive discipline, resentment is less likely to arise. Because after the positive disciplined is served, then the slate is wiped clean, and the child immediately has all the privileges he had before the infraction. Furthermore, a positive discipline can be implemented immediately; the time between the infraction and the consequence is greatly reduced. Studies have shown that disciplinary actions are most effective when they occur within 5 seconds of the inappropriate behavior (Schramm, 2006).

The importance of a fast reaction time is illustrated in how speeding tickets are distributed in Germany. In Germany, we have these cameras along the roadside. They are here and there and everywhere. If you dive by one over the speed limit, you see a sudden flash of red light, and you know you have been caught. What happens then? You slow down immediately. You know you will get a ticket with a remarkably clear picture of your face and license plate number. (We have them in the front back of the cars in Germany. The result is that you drive slower for the rest of the day and the days to follow, maybe for a week or two. But if you are a speeder, then eventually you will start driving just as fast as before. But the point is that as soon as one sees that red light flash, one hits the breaks immediately and drives at a slower tempo, even though one could keep driving just as fast, and it would have no effect on the speeding ticket already to come.

However, when the speeding ticket arrives, usually more than a month later, one's reaction to it is much different. Suddenly, you no longer feel the immediate influence of the red light, you are holding a 50 € or more bill in your hand, and your reaction changes from "darn, I was speeding" to "this stupid camera." Suddenly you are no longer at fault for speeding, but the camera is at fault for catching you. What has happened is that the punishment is so far removed from the moment of the behavioral infraction that the punishment leads only to resentment and not a behavior change.

Studies have also shown that punishment is not the most effective way to influence a child's behavior; reinforcement is. Imagine speeding tickets worked the other way around? What if we got a small reward for, say, every 10 kilometers we drove appropriately. If speeding and all other traffic laws reinforced good driving instead of punishing bad driving, then not only would we all drive better, but we would also like driving much more.

Let us apply this concept to the example of a child who is old enough to have learned to go to the bathroom when needed but often fails to do so when he is preoccupied with another reinforcement and perhaps even engages in an appropriate activity, such as playing. The child is playing and having fun, feels that he needs to go, but simply doesn't because he does not want to stop playing. So he keeps playing and wets his pants and then calls out to his mom. She comes and yells a bit while she takes his clothes, gives him new ones, and says no dessert for you tonight, while the child simply carries on playing and thinks, 'We'll see about that dessert thing later.' If one were to insert a positive punishment in this situation, the child's attitude might be significantly changed. For example, the child could the required to stop playing and then be made to wash out his underwear in the sink, then clean out the sink, and then take the dirty wet underwear to the dirty clothes hamper, and perhaps even do a load of laundry. Thus, his motivation not to go to the toilet and infringe on his playtime has backfired. Not only has he lost playtime, but he also has to do laundry too. But having done that, he can now go back to playing, and the question of dessert is not set up for a future argument. Positive punishment is more effective than negative punishment, but even more effective is positive reinforcement.

A positive reinforcement could be implemented in such a situation in the following manner: The parents of this child will certainly be aware of this problem. In passing by, they might notice that he is squeezing his legs together inconspicuously. Even if not, they could give him a prompt, "The bathrooms free now." "Is there anything you might need to do?" Having perhaps experienced the positive punishment previously, the child may very well get up and go to the toilet. If he returns from the toilet, finds some juice and a cookie, or some other kind of positive reinforcement, he will clearly understand going to the toilet on time is much better than not. Thus, the next time, the parents might hear, "I am going to the toilet, can I get a cookie?". Of course, this could and often does, lead to a smaller problem. The child may simply begin to go to the toilet whenever he wants a cookie. This may have to be addressed, but such is parenting: One problem at a time.

Parenting and Discipline

Discipline is a significant part of parenting. Nevertheless, many question how much discipline is necessary and if it may not be better for a child to be raised in an environment where he can make his own decisions a significant amount of the time. I am not of this opinion, but I want to be fair and point out this perspective; otherwise, some of my readers find me too harsh. Parenting methods that invoke the anti-discipline principal do so for a few reasons. First, such a method may tend to foster happiness. After all, when a child can essentially do whatever he wants, such a child would most likely be happy most of the time. However, what happens when a problem arises for a child. For example, he wants to go outside to play but cannot find his shoes, put them on, or tie them. Something almost every human being alive must do every day. In anti-disciplinary parenting, the method may not foster the proper learning skills and simply find the shoes, put them on the child, and tie them and send the child on its way. And that is what most of us as parents do in some way or another. And that is fine; after all, it is often in our interest that the child plays outside for awhile. But when we begin to live our lives for our child's happiness, we have to do more and more for the child to keep him happy. The child is happy, but how do we feel. Ok, some will say, 'my child's happiness is my happiness." Ok, I will even accept that. But what happens as the development continues under such anti-disciplinary parenting. We give out participation prizes because we do not want anyone to feel bad about losing. We buy another ice cream cone after the first one is dropped on the ground. We guard the child against any stress, frustration, sadness, and essentially anything we would not want to experience ourselves. What is the problem with that, you may ask? At some point, significantly later in life, a child raised with an anti-disciplinary parenting method will experience a problem that the parent cannot solve. Then it becomes the adult's problem and responsibility. The child's problems become the parent's problems, but at some point, each of us has to learn to find our shoes ourselves, put them on, and tie them ourselves.

The Bible has a quite different view of discipline. Often when I am talking with parents who find it difficult or even unnecessary to discipline their child, I ask them, "What is the duty of a parent?" Often the answer I get is to love their children. This may sound weird coming from a proclaimed Christian, but I disagree. The duty of a parent is to raise their children in love. In this context, Hebrews 12: 5 – 11 equates discipline with love. This passage points out quite clearly that God perceives us as His children. As such, He disciplines us out of love, and we should do the same with our children.

"And have you completely forgotten this word of encouragement that addresses you as a father addresses his son? It says, 'My son, do not make light of the Lord's discipline and do not lose heart when he rebukes you, 6because the Lord disciplines the one he loves, and he chastens everyone he accepts as his son' {Proverbs 3:11-12}. Endure hardship as discipline; God is treating you as his children. For what children are not disciplined by their father? If you are not disciplined – and everyone undergoes disciplined – then you are not legitimate, not true sons and daughters at all. Moreover, we have all had human fathers who disciplined us and respected them for it. How much more should we submit to the Father of spirits and live! They disciplined us for a little while as they thought best: but God disciplines us for our good, so that we may share in his holiness. No discipline seems pleasant at the time, but painful. Later on, however, it produces a harvest of righteousness and peace for those who have been trained by it.

When a child displays inappropriate behavior, then an act of discipline should follow, to teach the child that such behavior is inappropriate, as previously explained. However, when a child displays appropriate behavior, reinforcement must follow to teach the child that such behavior is appropriate. We do not want to see what we must discipline, and what we do want to see we must reinforce. As children of God, we live under the same construct in the form of natural and unnatural consequences.

This learning behavior that all humans have has been bestowed upon us by God. And as his children, he raises us in a similar but even more productive way. He does not punish us as if we were toddlers like He did in the times of Moses. Now He simply allows the consequences of our actions to follow. In 1. Corinthians 10:23 Paul writes," 'I have the right to do anything,' you say – but not everything is beneficial. 'I have the right to do anything' – but not everything is constructive" (NIV). Many see the Bible as a book of don'ts, but it is much more a book of dos. Jesus pointed this out very clearly when asked, "Of the commandments, which is the most important? Jesus replied: "Love the Lord you God with all your heart and with all your soul and with all of your mind and with all of your strength. ... Love your neighbor as yourself" (Mark 12:30-31, NIV). These are not don'ts; these are do's. People today tend to get so caught up in not doing the don'ts that they do not get around to doing the dos.

If you want to be happy and grow and experience fulfillment in your life, then concentrate on doing the do's, for God reinforces this behavior. I know this is much more easily said and done, and skeptics will say God is "jealous and proud of it; a petty, unjust, unforgiving control-freak; a vindictive, bloodthirsty ethnic cleanser; a misogynistic, homophobic, racist, infanticidal, genocidal, filicidal, pestilential, megalomaniacal, sadomasochistic, capriciously malevolent bully" (Dawkins, 2006, pg. 51). I can truly understand Dawkins's complaints. Just as I have previously explained, if one perceives all the bad in the world as an unjust discipline, resentment inevitably follows.

Prayer and Classical conditioning

I consider myself a man of God, but the concept of prayer is something that has eluded my understanding for many years until I viewed it from a psychological perspective. My dilemma was this; I could not understand why God has commanded us to pray for all things and at all times. If God is all-knowing, then he certainly knows what we want and need. If He is all-powerful, then He can surely deliver to us what we want and need. And if He is all-loving, then He will surely give us what we need without us having to ask for it continually. After all, if God's Will will be done, why should we have to pray that God will do what he will do anyway? Nevertheless, the Bible teaches very clearly that we should continue to pray and ask God for whatever we want (Ephesians 6:18); although, regardless of what, when, or how often we ask for something, God will either grant it or He will not; and that depends solely on His will, not ours. Even Jesus was refused a prayer request because the request was not according to God's will (Mark, 14:36).

This poses a difficult theological question because, on the concept of prayer, the Bible teaches us two basic things. First of all, do it. It is a commandment. We are called to pray and to do so often. Secondly,

God will do what He wants to do anyway. For the longest time, I simply accepted this as one of the many things to which we commonly respond, 'God works in mysterious ways.' However, when one addresses the concept of prayer from a psychological perspective, one sees that there is a distinct method in the madness.

Newberg and Waldman (2009) found that prayer changes the neuroplasticity (the structure and connections of brain cells) of our brains, which has been found to be beneficial to mental health. Thus, I would like to address this question from a psychological perspective and ask what happens when we pray. Generally, people pray for something they want. As I pointed out earlier in the discussion on learning behavior, when someone wants something, the potential for learning increases immensely. Thus, when we pray to God for things that we want, God can use this to teach us what we should want. That is, through prayer, God teaches us to want for ourselves exactly that what He wants for us. He does this through a concept that has become known in the field of scientific psychology as classic conditioning.

Classic Conditioning is quite simple, and contrary to popular belief, it is not how dogs learn or think. Rather, Pavlov merely discovered this type of learning through experiments with dogs and other vertebrates (Skinner, 1938; Clark, 2004). Classical conditioning is essentially the transfer of a particular behavior, associated with a specific stimulus, on to a different stimulus. Pavlov found that when a dog was presented with a nice juicy piece of meat, his mouth began to water. Then Pavlov began to first ring a bell and then present the dog with the food. After only a very short time, Pavlov noticed that the dog's mouth began to water as soon as it heard the bell rather than first at the sight of food.

It has since then been established that essentially all vertebrates can be taught through classical conditioning. In fact, this often happens without us even realizing it, and behaviors learned through classical conditioning can stay with us for a lifetime. When I was an undergraduate at Ohio University, we all became classically conditioned from the toilets when we were in the shower. Because when we were under the shower and then heard the toilet flush, we had about one second to get out of the water jet, or else one got scalded. To this day, when I am under a shower, and I hear a toilet flush, I still step out of the water jet to avoid getting burned.

So, what does this have to do with prayer requests? What does God want to teach us through classical conditioning through prayer? Let us go through it step by step. People generally pray for what they want, but quite often, God does not want for us the same things that we want for ourselves. Essentially God wants to teach us to want for ourselves the very same thing He wants for us. If that were the case, if we wanted for ourselves the very same thing that God wanted for us, then every prayer request would come into fulfillment.

But as it is, we often do not want for ourselves the things God wants for us. Through prayer requests, God can teach us, through classical conditioning, to want for ourselves the same thing that he wants for us. Thus, the more we pray, the more God can reveal His Will for our lives to us. To understand how this works, we have to introduce and define the concept of the pleasure principle. This simply states, and many scientific studies have confirmed that organisms tend to conduct actions that they have learned lead to pleasure and avoid actions that they have learned lead to pain.

As such, there are essentially two possible answers to a prayer request: yes, you get what you want, or No, you do not get what you want. When God tells us yes, that is such an amazingly wonderful feeling. We feel immensely loved and cared for; it is simply awesome. I dare say, having something wonderful happen for which I have prayed for specifically results in a significantly greater joy than when something wonderful happens that I did not pray for. Similarly, when our prayers are answered with a no, we are generally not so happy. Moreover, when we have specifically prayed for something, and God answers with a no, then, at least for me, the disappointment is coupled with a sense of reassurance that I have laid up my request to God, He has said no, and I simply accept His will, knowing that it is His will.

But when bad things happen, for which we had not prayed for at all or that had not been previously in our conscious awareness, we do become vividly aware of such problems as soon as they arise. At that time, we can then decide to either communicate our prayer requests to God or not. The difference is feedback.

If a person just goes through life, trusting in God for his well-being and livelihood, but without prayer. Such a man could indeed be well off, but He will live his life like a leaf blowing in the wind, having no idea of where his life is going. And the chances of him succumbing to significant fear and anxiety again are extremely high. But a person, who lifts up their prayer requests to God regularly, continually, and specifically receives feedback in terms of God's answers to these prayer requests. Thus, when God answers 'yes' in some situations, then we are encouraged in that direction, and when He answers 'no' in other situations, then we are discouraged in that direction. As such, prayer requests are not a means of getting what we want; they are a means of understanding what God wants for us. And the more prayer requests we offer up to Him, the more feedback we get, and hence the more we learn to want what God wants for us.

The pleasure principle suggests that humans, and essentially all organisms, instinctively do what makes them happy and avoid what makes them unhappy. Thus, because we want to have our prayers answered with a yes, we instinctively learn to pray for things according to the will of God. That is, we ask Him for the things that we think he wants for us, and we do not ask Him for the things that we do not think He wants for us. Then as we continue to pray throughout our lives, we get closer and closer to wanting for our lives the same things He wants for our lives.

Chapter Five

Faith, Hope, and Love

The Bible teaches, 'these three remain, faith, hope, and love, but the greatest of these is love.' In this section, I would like to first outline a psychological perspective of these three concepts, which for many people serve as life forces.

Faith

It is on the concept of faith in that science and theology differ perhaps most significantly. I have spent that last week reviewing scientific studies on the concept of faith; and, I venture to say that I may be able to guess what the authors' spiritual belief was, based on their presentation of the data. Some clearly wanted to show that faith was beneficial. Others wanted to show that faith was not so significantly beneficial. The data itself presents a totally different but equally difficult problem. How does one measure faith? I can imagine that some Christians would argue that faith in God is something that cannot be measured at all, for only God knows the heart and faith of man (1 Samuel 16:7).

Nevertheless, without measurement, there is no science. And since I am claiming to adopt a scientific viewpoint, I must address the concept of faith-based on scientific data. Various instruments of quantitative and qualitative measurement have been devised that attempt to measure the concept of faith. These instruments have been used in many studies that will now be outlined and reviewed.

Chatters' et al., (1992) Religiosity Scale measures the concept of faith base on factors such as religious attendance, private prayer, and importance of religion on a self-reported categorical measurement on a Likert scale (as cited in Ai, Wink, Tice, Bolling, and Shearer, 2009). Ai, Wink, Tice, Bolling, and Shearer (2009) and Ai, Wink, and Shearer (2011) proposed to measure spiritual experiences and sense of reverence quantitatively on a similar scale. Bekke-Hansen et al. (2012) measured faith based on denominations and diachronic variables based on yes/no answers to questions pertaining to the existence and nature of God. Kuilema (2014, pg. 157) offered a definition of true faith:

"True faith is not only a knowledge and conviction that everything God reveals in his Word is true; it is also a deep-rooted assurance, created in me by the Holy Spirit that, out of sheer grace earned for us by Christ, not only others, but I too, have had my sins forgiven, have been made forever right with God, and have been granted salvation."

This definition of faith differs significantly from the definition in works that address faith from a scientific direction. As such, Kuilema's definition of faith could not be measured with the means that other authors have used. One would be amazed at how many forms of measurement have been developed to measure the concept of faith. Bormann et al. (2006) implemented measurements using the Impact of Events Scale-Revised, Perceived Stress Scale, Anxiety Inventory, trait anger inventory-Short form, Center for epidemiological study-Depression Scale, and the Functional Assessment of Chronic Illness Therapy Spiritual Well-being-Expanded 4th Version (FACIT-SPEX-V4). Canada et al. (2013) also used the FACIT to conduct studies on racial and ethnic differences in spiritual well-being among cancer survivors. However, the validity and reliability of measurement as complex as these on oversimplified scales may be seriously questioned. Nevertheless, as difficult as the measurement may be, measurements must be made and generated into data; otherwise, one cannot claim to be science-based.

One way to compensate for this error in measurement is to increase the sample size. Francis and Liverpool (2009) did this in their review of the empirical literature on faith and found that faith-based programs have proven to be significantly beneficial. The benefits of faith as it pertains to health are widely supported. Canada et al. (2013) found that religion and spirituality are vital resources employed by survivors of cancer to cope with the illness and its treatment. Holt-Lunstad, Steffen, Sandberg, and Jensen (2011) demonstrated an association between spiritual well-being and better health. Newlin, Dyess, Allard, Chase, and Mulkus (2011) argued that spirituality and religion may be related to effective diabetes self-management. Tsai and Rosenheck (2011) suggested that religious beliefs and practices are commonly helpful for people with severe mental illness.

On the other hand, many studies have come to different conclusions. Sherman, Simonton, Latif, Spohn, and Tricot (2004) examined general religiousness and found that patients' typical involvement in religion was not linked to psychosocial or physical functioning. Ai, Wink, and Shearer (2011) explored the role of both traditional and secular religiousness and reverence in postoperative hospital length of stay and found that a significant relationship between faith and health was unlikely to be moderated by a combination of various variables and not from variables independence from each other. Pedersen, Christensen, Jensen, and Zachariae (2013) suggested that some patients may view their cancer as a punishment from God, believe that God has an intended meaning with their cancer, or see religious faith as a potential curative factor. Their faith may thereby influence their decision-making regarding treatment in both beneficial and potentially harmful ways.

Still, others have concluded that the measurement of the concept of faith is so complex that any conclusions derived from the analysis of data should still be reviewed with scrutiny (Tsai and Rosenheck, 2011; Newlin, Dyess, Allard, Chase, and Mulkus (2011). Bekke-Hansen et al. (2012) suggested that religious faith and spiritual faith should be perceived separately because people can be spiritual without being religious and vice versa. Bormann et al. (2006) suggested that both religious and spiritually-based practices are associated with better health outcomes, improved quality of life, reduced stress, reduced hypertension, improved pain management, improved cerebral blood flow, and EEG changes. However, it was noted that many of these studies were not peer-reviewed. Canada et al. (2013) suggested that the concepts of religion and spirituality are multifaceted and overlapping constructs whose definitions and distinctions are subjected to continual debate.

In reference to Aristotle, faith as a virtue was explained by first defining virtue as the ideal balance between too much or too little of any given attribute. For example, bravery is the middle point between folly and cowardice (as cited in Kuilema, 2014). Nevertheless, the scientific psychological perspective of the concept of faith may not significantly coincide with the Christian perspective of faith. Chappell (1996) was cited with the statement that the status of faith as a virtue is predicated on the existence of God, for if God does not exist, faith is not a virtue. And if God does exist, He clearly does not want our faith to sway in a midpoint between two extremes (Revelation 3:15). As such, this concept, in its limiting manner, may not fit the Christian understanding in which a middle point is not good enough. John Calvin (1996) was quoted,

"We shall now have a full definition of faith if we say that it is a firm and sure knowledge of the divine favor toward us, founded on the truth of a free promise in Christ, and revealed to our minds, and sealed on our hearts, by the Holy Spirit.

My idea of faith has been lent to me by a poster that I brought home from Sunday school one day many years ago. It was a picture of a cute little kitten, who was hanging from the handle of an Easter basket by one single claw and about to fall into the basket. The caption read, "faith isn't faith until it is all you are holding on to." Such a view of faith may be better described as a state of mind and may, therefore, not lend itself to be measured based on the means previously described. In his description of the nature of science, Einstein has been quoted with a definition of insanity as doing the same thing repeatedly and expecting different results. If this is the case, then faith may be the exact opposite.

There is even a term for the concept of faith in the field of science; it is call bias. Bias arises when a scientist has formulated a theory or hypothesis or supports a particular theory or hypothesis and wants to demonstrate that this theory or hypothesis is true. However, the mere fact that the scientist is claiming relevance of a particular theory suggests that the scientist also believes this theory, for no one would base work time and effort on a concept they did not believe to be true. Hence, in ethics classes, scientists are warned to take distinct actions and care that their work not be tainted with biases.

At the end of the day, the scientist, as well as the theologian, have to be content with the belief that that which he believes to know is also actually true. But what is the theological perspective on the concept of faith? In Hebrews 11, Paul offers a very good and useful definition of faith, followed by many descriptive examples. "Now faith is confidence in what we hope for and assurance about what we do not see. This is what the ancients were commended for. By faith, we understand that the universe was formed at God's command so that what is seen was not made out of what was visible" (Hebrew 11:1-3, NIV). Paul then continues by offering examples of faith, as demonstrated by Abel, Enoch, Noah, Abraham, Isaac, and Jacob, Sarah, Joseph, Moses, Joshua, and Rehab, outlining each of their acts of faith. Paul concludes by stating that the list goes on and on with honorable mentions of Gideon, Barak, Samson, and Jephthah, about David and Samuel and the prophets.

If you have not already, I strongly suggest that you look up the above characters and read their stories of great faith for yourselves. Each of them has in common the acceptance of the promise God gave to each of them. They had no reason to believe that God would do what He promised each of them. In fact, in each of the above examples, God's promise to them was so far fetched that it challenged their rational thought processes. Nevertheless, they had faith that God would do what He said He would, and that was all they were holding on to.

The above examples are examples of God's specific promises to specific people; however, He promises each of us, all humanity, something as well: Eternal life. He may promise each of us individually specific things, but eternal life with Him in Heaven is his promise to all humankind. Ephesians 2:8 states that "For it is by grace you have been saved, through faith – and this is not from yourselves, it is the gift of God. If you believe that Jesus Christ died on the cross in payment for your sins and you accept this gift with the same certainty that the ground will support your next step under your feet then, this is the faith that God wants us to have. This is the kind of faith that has the power to move mountains (Matthew 21:21).

I know this seems far fetched, and many have discussed whether this is to be taken literally or metaphorically, but James 1:3 challenges us to test this faith. Furthermore, James points out that faith is not only a state of mind or emotion but rather a way of life that is defined by our actions and behaviors. An anecdote that I have heard my father tell quite often explains what is meant in James 2:14-17, "What good is it, my brothers and sisters if someone claims to have faith but has no deeds? Can such faith save them? Suppose a brother or a sister is without clothes and daily food. If one of you says to them, "Go in peace; keep warm and well fed," but does nothing about their physical needs, what good is it? In the same way, faith by itself, if it is not accompanied by action, is dead."

As the story goes, a man named Blondin walked over the Niagara falls in 1860. He walked back and forth, upping the ante in difficulty each time, performing various stunts in the middle. To cut to the chase, he proceeded to fill a wheelbarrow with water and balanced the sluggish apparatus back and forth with the utmost of ease. Upon having done this and many other stunts, demonstrating his unfailing balance, he asked the crowded, "Who thinks I can do it one more time?" The crowd applauded with encouragement, for the question seemed almost rhetorical after he had done the feat so often already. But he asked again, "Does anybody believe I can do it one more time?" Again the crowd replied with cheers of affirmation. But then, as Blondin added, "Ok if you all believe I can do it again, I will ask you, who will get in the wheelbarrow?"

If you do not get into God's wheelbarrow, then your faith is not all you are holding on to.

Hope

The concept of hope may not seem to be something that scientific psychologists spend much time studying and researching. This is not due to a lack of importance on the subject but rather due to the difficulty of grasping it by scientific psychological means. Haugan, Utvær, and Moksnes (2013) defined hope as "the act by which the temptation of despair is actively overcome and has thus been interpreted as an inner strength and an available resource for living in the present" (p.378). These authors suggested that the concept of hope is essential to well being in nursing home settings. To investigate this, the Herth Hope Index, a measure of an individual's level of hope on three factors, (a.) temporality and future, (b.) positive readiness and expectancy, and (c.) interconnectedness, was developed as a means of quantifying individuals' levels of hope. This measure of an individual's hope is widely used. It has been tested and found to exhibit good reliability and validity to concepts such as self-transcendence, spiritual well-being, purpose in life, depression, and anxiety. This demonstrates that hope is important to well-being from a psychological perspective and the concept of hope has been thoroughly studied employing scientific psychological methods. Understanding that an abstract, intangible, and essentially unobservable concept such as hope cannot be justly investigated by quantitative procedures alone, Holtslander, Duggleby, Williams, and Wright (2005) used qualitative methods to gain a greater understanding of the concept of hope. These authors defined hope simply as an inner strength that gives one the courage and the ability to go through a difficult situation and concluded that hope is an essential part of living.

Viktor Frankl may have been one of the first psychologists to understand the crucial importance of hope in people's lives. He wrote, "If there is purpose in life at all, there must be a purpose in suffering and death. But no man can tell another what this purpose is. Each must find out for himself, and must accept the responsibility that his answer prescribes." (Frankl, 1959, *Man's Search for Meaning*, Page 11)

The story of Viktor Frankl is truly an amazing one. In his book, "Man's search for meaning," Frankl tells how he came to the understanding that hope is essentially what keeps us alive. Incidentally, his book, except for perhaps the Bible, is the book I have suggested most often for my clients to read. His story is incredible, and without spoiling too much of it for the reader now, it is important to set the stage.

Frankl had a manuscript for his book on psychotherapy when the nazis caught him and threw him in a concentration camp. He seemed to have more concern for his manuscript than for his own life and kept the manuscript on his body, looking for a trustworthy face with whom he could entrust his life's work, knowing that they would eventually find it, take it away, and burn it. He spots a guard that he had a good enough feeling about to trust him to get his book to safety. So he leans out of line and whispers to a guard that he has something very valuable with him and tries to hand over the book to him inconspicuously. But the guard simply ripped the book out of his hand and threw it in the garbage.

And so his life's work, his personally developed therapeutic method, was lost and gone forever. And not only that, to make matters worse, he was in a Nazi concentration camp on top of that as well! With his life's work gone and lost forever, and a dismal future and an even more horrid present, Frankl, from that point on, only concentrated on survival. But as a psychologist, he could not help but take mental note of the behaviors of those around him, which he later comprised to *"Man's search for meaning."* The book tells a little about his daily life in the concentration camp, but one particular observation is relevant to our topic of hope. Frankl noticed that when a prisoner had lost hope, they smoked their hidden cigarettes instead of saving them for a moment when they had to trade them for something life important, like bribing a guard for food or medicine.

He writes, "In the concentration camp every circumstance conspires to make the prisoner lose his hold. All the familiar goals in life are snatched away. What alone remains is 'the last of human freedoms'– the ability to 'choose one's attitude in a given set of circumstances.'... The prisoners were only average men, but some, at least, by choosing to be 'worthy of their suffering' proved man's capacity to rise above his outward fate" (pg. 12).

Frankl observed that when a prisoner lost hope and came to the conclusion that their life had no more worth and was not worth living. They gave themselves up to their circumstances and consequently died shortly after. This observation sparked the grounding theory of Logo Therapy. Here the term Logo refers to its Latin translation of 'meaning' and not the more modern interpretation of 'logo' as short for logic or logical.

Frakl tells of his dialogues with various clients suffering from depression and suicidal thoughts. He would ask them a question, which came to me as a great surprise as a mental health practitioner myself when I first read it. He asked them why they have not killed themselves yet. While the question is no doubt very provocative, and provocation is not normally deemed acceptable in working with suicidal clients, the answer to this question offers knowledge of the client's still existing meaning or purpose in life. That is, the reason why the clients had not yet killed themselves is the reason they had to live. Having helped the client make this discovery, this purpose could be made into a ladder on which the client could climb out of their darkness.

Thus, the general goal of Frankl's Logotherapy is to help clients find their meaning and purpose in life. In my work with children with developmental disorders and their families, I also realized that if the parents did not see any purpose in their underdeveloped child's lives, they were not able to cope with the situations that inevitably arise through their circumstances, nor were they able to effectively foster their child's development in a way that maximized their child's potential.

The therapeutic method I used in this work, applied behavioral analysis (ABA), is often regarded as too harsh and demanding on the child. And honestly, at times, it does seem that way, for the nature of the method asserts little concern for a child's immediate happiness, which often leads to tears in many cases. When that happens, if the parents have too little hope that their child has any significant potential, they often choose to be content with simply keeping their child happy rather than exposing their child to the pain and suffering associated with the necessary work to reach one's potential. In short, learning to overcome is perhaps the most painful thing that anyone will ever endure. Moreover, it is a pain and struggle that every single person, without exception, will have to bear someday.

For this reason, most of the scientific psychological studies on the concept of hope are generally associated with death in some way. However, it is thoroughly conceivable that hope is not only an important concept in old age or illness but rather hope is a significant part of our daily lives throughout our whole lives. In fact, the book you are reading now is a testament to my conviction that no psychological therapeutic method will ever have any significant success if the client has no significant amount of hope. Even Nietzsche, who was critical of religion, still claimed that "He who has a Why to live can bear with almost any How."

At this point, a distinction must be made between the terms or concepts' hope for something' and 'hope in something,' a distinction that scientific psychology has failed to make. Regarding my previous statement, I would say that a significant amount of hope for something is sufficient for many therapeutic applications. If a person has hope for overcoming an ailment, regardless of how realistic this hope is, I would suggest that this person will have significantly more success than if they had no hope for recovery. The undisputed placebo effect is empirical evidence of this. The placebo effect has demonstrated that when individuals think that they are receiving a beneficial supplement of some kind, they feel and demonstrate a significant improvement, even though the given supplement is entirely neutral.

I would argue that individuals, who have their hope in God, may have an even greater 'hope strength' than individuals who have hope for something like a new car, popularity, a perfect relationship, or anything that they might want for themselves so bad that they would strive to get it. The difference these two prepositions make is quite intricate. Having hope for something means that something is missing or out of place, and one hopes that this will be corrected. However, hope in something takes a much larger scale. This means that regardless of what is missing or out of place, one hopes not specifically that it will all be corrected but rather that it will not be so important in the long run.

Diagnostic systems are used to classify and arrange psychological disorders based on their clinical symptoms. In a pyramid model, anxiety and depression would be at the bottom. Essentially everybody has episodes of depression and anxiety throughout their lives. As such, anxiety and depression are completely natural and even necessary conditions. Problems only occur if such episodes are either significantly frequent, intense, or long-lasting. If these conditions go untreated for a significant amount of time, they are likely to develop into other more severe symptoms.

From a spiritual perspective, one could define anxiety simply as the loss of hope that God will/can provide for us, and depression as a loss of hope that God wants to provide for us. Thus the spiritual mentality of anxiety is that God is not able to help us, and we are in this world on our own, and it is up to us to endure or die. The spiritual mentality of depression is that we are unworthy of help, and we are in this world on our own, and it is up to us to endure or die. Either way, life is a constant struggle for survival, and it is understandable how some may come to view life as a struggle, which ultimately everyone loses.

Thus, to some degree, the importance of hope and religion may be to gather up enough hope to establish the core belief that they are not in the world completely alone and are worthy of being alive. If one can develop some purpose in their life, they will probably have enough hope to get through most of the hardships life has to throw at them.

In my case, I do not have much hope for a cure for my physical illness. I encourage the scientists to keep working on it, but I am not holding my breath that they will be successful in my lifetime, if ever at all. But I do have great hope in God, that whether or not I am healed in this life, I will nevertheless prosper here in this life because "The Lord is my shepherd, I lack nothing. He makes me lie down in green pastures, he leads me beside quiet waters, he refreshes my soul. He guides me along the right paths for his name's sake. Even though I walk through the darkest valley, I will fear no evil, for you are with me; your rod and your staff, they comfort me. You prepare a table before me in the presence of my enemies. You anoint my head with oil; my cup overflows. Surely your goodness and love will follow me all the days of my life, and I will dwell in the house of the Lord forever" (Psalms 23:1-6, NIV).

Love

Contrary to the popular assumption, love is not an emotion or a feeling (Ekman, 2015). Ekman explained that emotions are only temporary effects that may last only a single moment and rarely more than an hour at a time. Therefore, love is a state of mind that persists for much longer periods, years at a time, even an entire lifetime. Furthermore, emotions and feelings are, as previously discussed, somatic responses to emotionally provoking stimuli. That is, emotion is in response to something, while love need not be provoked into existence, but rather is constantly there regardless of perceived stimuli. In short, emotion is because of something, while love simply is.

Nevertheless, it is easy to understand how one could assume that love is an emotion because when one is in a love state of mind, one may indeed experience significantly more emotional episodes than when one is not "in love." But still, what is love? A search of scientific psychological research on the topic of love yielded 73,235 entries on the ProQuest Psychology database. Mary Hotvedt, President of the American Association for Marriage and Family Therapy, suggested that the answer to this question is subjective and depends on a person's perception of love, their current associations with love, their current situation, and state of mind. Sexologist John Money from the society for the scientific study of sexuality agreed that culture and society offers a comprehensive understanding of the concept of love that may vary across gender, age, culture, class, and many other variables.

On the other hand, the executive director of the American Philosophical Association dared a more concise definition: "Love between human beings is the emotional bond of those who find meaning and value in the aspects of life." While this definition may be concise and thus more useful, when one then asks, what is an emotional bond, the matter gets very complicated very fast. While emotions do tend to cause bonding of sorts, the bonding of a shared emotion certainly does not always indicate the presence of love or have a cause and effect relationship with love. If this were the case, people who saw the same movie together in a movie theater and experienced similar emotions could be described as being in love with each other, which is absurd. Still, one may be more inclined to smile at the people sitting in the vicinity after the movie is over than before the movie had begun. Still, people who see a movie together, regardless of how good or emotional it is, do not generally fall in love at first sight after the movie is over. However, 'love at first sight' instances do generally happen when the two people are sharing an emotional moment. Still, one would not easily argue that the short emotional bond caused them to fall in love, but would most likely attribute the love connection to many other factors.

Similarly, Fink (2015) illustrated the diversity in the kinds of problems that love can induce and the psychological repercussions of these various kinds of problems. Ahmetoglu, Swami, and Chamorro-Premuzic (2010) attempted to measure various aspects of love empirically. These authors write, "As an abstract concept, love is typically taken to represent a range of human emotions, from simple feelings of pleasure to overwhelming and ineffable attraction towards another person. Therefore, it is not surprising that the subject of the concept of love has long been the muse of poets and songwriters (Berscheid, 1988). At the same time, the concept of love is of increasing interest in the psychological sciences. Psychologists have approached the topic of love from many different perspectives, including biochemistry (e.g., Emanuele et al., 2006), evolutionary psychology (e.g., Buss, 1999), psychoanalysis (Gordon, 2006), and theology (e.g., Tjeltveit, 2006). It is only more recently that psychologists have focused on the pivotal role of individual differences in love and relationship quality, examining such variables as physical attractiveness (Swami, Stieger, Haubner, Voracek, & Furnham, 2009), attitudinal dispositions (Feng & Baker, 1994), and emotional intelligence (Zeidner & Kaluda, 2008). Thus, while these authors also essentially demonstrate that the concept of love is too abstract to measure quantitatively, one cannot operate scientifically without observing, recording, and analyzing data of some kind. Thus, these authors set out to examine the associations between love, personality, and relationship length. As one may have expected, these authors found that age was negatively associated with passion and positively associated with intimacy and commitment. Agreeableness was positively associated with love, and passion was negatively associated with relationship length. So, what does this tell us? It confirms what most people already know about love. Young love is wild and fleeting, while mature love is less passionate but more enduring.

This research of scientific psychological studies on the concept of love enticed me to conclude that the concept of love simply exceeds the capacity of human understanding. Love seems like an emotion but does not at all fit into the scientific definition of emotion. It can be measured, but only in explicitly defined facets. These facets are many and overlap so much that one must question the reliability and validity of measurements. When love is measured, even in the most exact way possible, the conclusions are little more than confirmation of what we already know from listening to the Beatles or reading Shakespeare's sonnets. Thus, although love is a major reason why individuals seek professional psychological help and love has even been described as malice toward mental health (Fink, 2015), scientific psychology has failed to reach a consensus of what love is and what should be done about it.

The Bible's definition of love differs from the definitions derived from scientific psychology in that it not only describes what love is but also describes what love is not. When you think about it, this makes perfect sense and is probably something scientific psychology should have learned by now. After all, the diversity of the concept of love has been more than well established. Thus, one could conclude that it is not sufficient to talk about what love is, but rather one must also address what love is not. 1. Corinthians 13: 4-8) defines love like this: "Love is patient, love is kind. It does not envy, it does not boast, it is not proud. It does not dishonor others, it is not self-seeking, it is not easily angered, it keeps no record of wrongs. Love does not delight in evil but rejoices with the truth. It always protects, always trusts, always hopes, always perseveres. Love never fails..."

With this description of love, it is easy to see that love, as it is described here, is not passion, lust, or romance. It is not a desire of wanting but rather a desire of giving. Love is not something one needs to have, but rather something one needs to give. Love does not lead to hurt, but only to healing. Passion, lust, desire, romance, and the like are often associated or even equated with love, these things can and do indeed cause hurt and pain, but love, pure love, does not.

Think about someone you love for a moment and examine all the many facets of the various emotions and feelings you have for this person. I will wait while you do that. Ok, now, subtract from those feelings everything that may be associated with a want, a need, or a desire. What is left over? If there is not much left over, then the love may not be very pure. But, if, after subtracting the wants, needs, and desires, one finds oneself with a basket full of nurture, compassion, admiration, warmth, and other such attributes that project giving rather than taking, then one may be confident that the love is significantly pure. And so if all the love giving attributes are in there, a little bit of lust and desire is much less likely to spoil it all.

CHAPTER SIX

Living and Growing in the Holy Spirit

As a psychologist who has worked extensively in the field of child development, it is very interesting to consider the child development of Jesus. Without diving into a complex theological discussion, let me formulate a scientific assumption, from which the following discussion will follow. Jesus, being fully human, has undergone the same developmental process as all of us. In addition to that, he was subjected to the same emotionally provocative stimuli as all of us. He was fully and completely human, with the same 46 chromosome gnome that we have. Only 23 of them came from His mother and the other 23 from, ... well from God. Now, that is a debate, just waiting to explode, but when all is said and done, Jesus had to somehow end up with 46 chromosomes; otherwise, he would not have been human. So, where the Chromosomes came from is not the question; the question is, what made Jesus different from the rest of us. How was he able to live a sin-free life. I would suggest it was His Spirit. Jesus was conceived with the Spirit of God, right from the very beginning. All of his early childhood developmental processes took place while already being fulling filled with the Spirit of God. As a human baby, he would not have even been able to conceive this at a level of conscious awareness; nevertheless, it was there all through His childhood development.

It is hard to understand what that means. Let me try to spell it out for you. Living and walking in the Holy Spirit is something that we as adults at some point begin to try to do after we accept Jesus as our Lord and Savior, but Jesus had it right from the git-go. And so, at the point where babies cognitively understand who their parents are, and their identity development begins to set it. Jesus underwent the same process, only that he was already then filled with the Holy Spirit and communicated to God the Father through it. That would no doubt have a positive effect on emotional, cognitive, and all other developmental processes. But what also makes Jesus unique among humans is his mind. For while you, I, and everyone else grew up to be who they are today, Jesus grew up to become who he had always been. Jesus's divinity existed through his mind, which was God's mind through the Holy Trinity. People may often wish they could speak to their teenage self as the adult they were today. Jesus could essentially do exactly that.

I am coming up fast on the 50 years maker, and I am just beginning to understand what it means to be empowered. Normally it takes a lifetime for one to become truly connected to the Holy Spirit. Imagine if the connection was already fully complete at the moment of conception. Sure, one would have the same hardships in life like everybody else, but being already fully empowered by the Holy Spirit might take a bit of the sting out of puberty, to say the least.

If we examine the development of Jesus' heart, body, mind, and soul in light of his interconnection with the Holy Spirit, one may gain a greater understanding of who He is. To begin with, Jesus' body was not different than yours or mine. And his physical development was also the same as ours. However, the development of his heart, mind, and soul may have been significantly different. Jesus was not only connected to the Father through the Holy Spirit; He was indeed part of the Father. John 1: 1-14 illustrates that Jesus did not come into existence at his birth, like the rest of us do, but rather Jesus had existed from the beginning and even played a significant role in the creation of the universe. As such, his soul was essentially fully and perfectly developed upon conception, which would have undoubtedly had a significant positive influence on his emotional and mental developmental processes, which may have been more like an exploration rather than a struggle. Jesus did not have to develop an identity and become the person he eventually became. Since the beginning of time, his identity was established, but he had let this identity unfold in human form after being born. That is, is His mind had to learn the Torah. He had to learn how to communicate effectively; and, He had to learn to deal with His human emotions, just like we do.

As I pointed out earlier, both the Bible and scientific psychology concur that humans are made up of heart, body, mind, and soul. These four components are confined to the boundary of the skin. They do not leave the body, at least not really, and not as long as the body is alive. One can let one's mind and thoughts to drift or have a so-called out of body experience, but such experiences and indeed all experiences occur in the mind, which is powered by the brain; no brain – no mind. And since the brain is clearly encapsulated in the skull, it can not wander off, but at least colloquially, the mind can wander off and get lost. One may have feelings of such experiences, but let us not confuse dreams with reality. Also, as defined in this work, one's soul is confined to the physical boundaries of the body. A very good or very bad soul may seem to have a projection onto others when we are in their vicinity. However, this is, again, a subjective feeling. No scientific or even theological evidence suggests that a person's soul (or goodness or moral – whatever you choose to call it) actually leaves the body. At least not while the body is still alive.

The Human Spirit, on the other hand... Well, first, let us define what we mean by Human Spirit. The American Heritage Dictionary defines the human spirit as the vital principle, the animating force traditionally believed to be within and the essential nature of every human being. Often associated with terms such as 'intrinsic motivation' and 'religious spirituality,' the human spirit was popularized in the 1980s to describe a wide-ranging set of beliefs and practices. Growing from the 1960s and 70s US counterculture, a new age movement maintains that a spiritual era is dawning to which individuals and whole societies will be transformed. However, White (2001) added that the human spirit adds wisdom, through values and ethics, to intelligence. Steiner (1918) argued that each human's spirit is the driving force in their purpose in life. In her dissertation concerning the childhood experience of ADHD, Redfern (2012) claimed that "Our spirit beckons us to heal and oneness with creation itself.

Similarly, Seaward suggested that Western science has ignored the essence and significance of human spirituality in the health and healing process. Our spirit is something we adopt and through which we identify our innermost core belief. The spirit is not something we are born with. It is something we take up later by choice after significant development of the heart, body, mind, and soul. Only after the spirit has been adopted does it begin to develop in an individual. But this spiritual development is contingent on the development of the individual's heart, body, mind, and soul. In the case of the Holy Spirit, which sets within us a core belief that Jesus Christ is Lord, through which we are identified as Christians. Only after significant spiritual development can the Holy Spirit have an empowering effect in our lives, by helping us make the right decisions and by helping us control our thoughts and feelings.

Proverbs 4:23 teaches, "Above all else guard your heart, for everything you do flows from it." And Colossians 3:1-2 directs us to, "... set your hearts on things above, where Christ is, seated at the right hand of God. Set your minds on things above, not on earthy things." Curiously, the principles of psychotherapy make similar suggestions. Psychology has found that what is in our hearts greatly influences what is in our minds. For example, if someone feels fat, it will not take very long until they also think they are fat. However, the reverse is also true. If a person thinks they are fat, it will not take long until they feel fat. So what is in the mind flows to the heart, and what is in the heart flows to the mind. This, in turn, influences behavior. If I think I am fat, I am going to feel fat, and then I am going to act fat. I will sit and slouch, become inactive, and eat potato chips for dinner because what is the difference? I am already fat. If I do these behaviors long enough, then I will develop habits; and if these habits persist long enough, then these habits will form my personality. And when we get to that point, change is extremely difficult. And after working as long as I have in this field, I have come to realize that change at this point is not only difficult but without the spirit of God essentially impossible.

It seems that scientific psychology attempts to encode how the heart and mind work together, but when I read the psychology of the Bible, it seems that it attempts to explain how they work apart. Again and again, the Bible explains how to catch bad thoughts before they affect the heart and how to catch bad feelings before they affect the mind. This is done by setting them both on God but separately. We set our minds on God, and we set our hearts on God. That gives us a backup. If we sin in our hearts (entertain bad feelings), we know that there is forgiveness, mercy, grace, and salvation. If we sin in our minds (entertain bad thoughts), we still feel God's love through the Holy Spirit, and we feel conviction and comfort, understanding, and love. And so we gain the power to stop bad thoughts and feelings before they affect our behavior to the point that habits are developed. That is the empowering effect of the Holy Spirit. Romans 5: 3-4,

> "... we also glory in our sufferings, because we know that suffering produces perseverance; perseverance, character; and character, hope. And hope does not put us to shame, because God's life has men poured out into our hearts through the Holy Spirit, who has been given to us."

Thus, when we are sad and bummed out beyond all control and be eating a bag of Doritos and a pint of cookie caramel swirl ice cream for dinner, we have the power to renew our minds, every day, day for day. And if you keep this up, this behavior, of turning to God, again and again, being renewed daily, this behavior becomes our habit. If we divulge in this habit long enough, it becomes our personality.

Chronic Illness

As I explained in the introduction of this book, in 1999, I was diagnosed with Emery Dreifuss Syndrome, a form of Muscular Dystrophy that leads to death in about two years. As you might imagine, this was a tremendous shock that completely changed my life. At that time, I had just begun working in children's hospitals as a clinic clown. During that time, I heard someone say to someone, "you can either live with an illness or you can die with it." I cannot remember who said this to whom or why, but it seemed to pack a lot of truth and quickly became part of my repertoire of inspiring words that I passed on to others as Dr. Clou, my clown name. I had probably said it ten times to various people before I got my diagnosis and realized how ridiculously easy it was to say and how difficult it was to live out. How does one live with a chronic and progressive illness?

First of all, I should explain, in case you are wondering how I may be still alive. There are two explanations for that. The doctors made a mistake and gave me the wrong diagnosis, or a miracle occurred. As it is, I clearly have some form of MD, most likely FSH, but I have never had an exact diagnosis done. Now at 49 years of age, my arms are more or less useless, but my hands still work well enough to type. I can stand for a minute or two at a time and walk 100 meters at a time. But it is getting worst. Slowly but surely, my physical strength is leaving me. So what does the Bible say about chronic Physical Illnesses, and what does psychology say about it.

The field of psychology attempts to approach the issue with an abundance of empathy, understanding, encouragement, support, and coping methods. All of which can be very helpful if carried out thoughtfully. While working as a clinic clown in various hospitals throughout Germany, I have heard doctors, nurses, psychologists, and even friends and families say these words, or something very similar, "I know how you feel." I have heard these words many times myself and no doubt said them also, but that was before I realized how incredibly dumb that sounds to someone struggling with chronic illness. The truth is that no one can ever know what someone else is feeling, regardless of their wisdom, experience, or knowledge. On Facebook, I am a member of a support group for individuals with FSH. It is extremely helpful. Members can ask questions about how others cope with various life situations. Everything from which sex positions work best to how to tackle stairs has been addressed in the group, but not once do I recall anyone replying, "Oh, I know how you feel." These are people all with the same disease-fighting with the same symptoms, but still, no one claims to know how someone else feels, who is in the same situation fighting the same disease. Instead, people reply more along these lines, "Oh yes, that is tough. This is what I have found works best for me..."

Claiming to know how someone feels is not helpful. It is belittling. I know it is meant well when someone tells me that, but it is simply not true. It is simple mathematics. Where $A \neq B$, $A+X \neq B+X$. If that is not convincing, try this. Take your shoes and socks off and put your feet close together. Now drop a brick on your feet so that it hits both of your big toes. And now examine the pain. The pain in both feet may be equally painful and feel the same, but it is still not the same pain. Each foot will have its own pain, even though they are both connected to the same body. How much more different will the pain be in two different bodies?

Nevertheless, people with chronic illness, here people saying to them, and meaning it well and with only the best intentions, "I know how you feel." This is commonly referred to as empathy. However, Carl Rogers, the definition of empathy is much more accurate. Carl Rogers (2007, pg. 243) defined empathy as the ability "to sense the client's private world as if it were your own, but without ever losing the AS IF quality." This AS IF quality is more important than one may imagine; and, I dare say this may be a quality that is extremely difficult to obtain. Psychologists and doctors, and other health professionals of great wisdom and knowledge, may though their experience may have a great understanding of a client's situation and illness based on their experience. But having a vast knowledge of a disease does not mean they have any knowledge of anyone with that disease. Thus individuals seeking medical or psychological help due to a chronic illness must, unfortunately, often take it upon themselves to filter information regarding one's illness and information regarding one's person.

No one can ever know how anyone else really and truly feels, and claiming to do so is, in my opinion, arrogant. For this reason, I never tell my clients, "I know how you feel," even when I may have a very good idea of how they might feel. Instead, I express this as a goal as a continuation. When insight has been obtained through therapy, I still only claim, "I am beginning to understand a little how you may feel." However, the Bible teaches us that God knows us better than we know ourselves. This is illustrated in Psalms 139, Isaiah 43, Jeremiah 1, John 10, Luke 12. As such, if one believes the Word of God, then one must also believe that God not only knows the clinical symptoms of our chronic illness but also knows how we feel due to our chronic illness.

I must say I have had as many bad experiences from other Christians concerning my illness than I have had good experiences. I have had people tell me my illness is due to my sin or my parent's sin. God would have healed me, but I lack faith, and other such forms of it are my fault that I am ill or still ill. In Chapter 6 of his book, *God Wants You Well*, Andrew Wommack seemed to suggest that God wants everyone to be healed, and in fact, has already healed them, but they have failed to receive the healing. I have a problem with that for two reasons. First, it does not coincide with the Theological logic of the following three truths: God is all-powerful, God is all-loving, and there is sickness in this world. The first two statements we believe to be true based on faith, the Bible's teaching, and the intercessions of the Holy Spirit. And the third, we know to be true. There is obviously sickness in the world. Andrew Wommack and many others I have come across have told me that my illness, nor any illness is God's will. If that were true, then God could not be both all-powerful and all-loving, and illness still be in the world. For if that were the case that it was not God's will that I have MD, then God could either be all-loving or all-powerful but not both. That is, either He is all Loving and does not want me to be ill, but since I clearly am, then He must not have the power to heal me. Or He has the power to heal me but just does not want to; therefore, He cannot be all-loving.

Secondly, Exodus 4-11 (NIV) points out that God himself claimed responsibility for the illnesses in the world, "The Lord said to him, 'Who gave humans beings their mouths? Who makes them deaf or mute? Who gives them sight or makes them blind? Is it not I, the Lord?" This was in response to Moses' excuse to send someone else to Pharaoh because Moses seemed to have some sort of speech impediment. God could have responded by simply saying, "Oh well, then let me just fix that right up," and just like that, Moses would have had a voice the made James Earl Jones sound like a squeaky teenager. But instead of healing Moses, he sent him to do Pharaoh as he was. When one looks at some of the Biblical heroes, almost all of them had some sort of problem.

I am not saying God does not heal or cannot heal. He can, and He does. I am saying that in some cases, he simply chooses not to because the illness that one person may suffer can serve for the ultimate good. The Bible is full of such examples. In Romans 8-28, it clearly states that "in all things, God works for the good of those who love him, who have been called according to his purpose." I am certainly not glad I have MD, but this is the way God created me. I know some will protest to that statement severely and claim sickness only comes from the devil. Well, besides the Exodus 4 verse, there is another line of thought that should be considered. Many would agree with the statement that only God can create life. The devil cannot create life or anything else for that matter; he can only destroy. Genetic illnesses such as MD occur at the moment of conception; at the moment, life begins. As such, I did not become sick at some time during life, but this genetic disorder was there the moment the 23 chromosomes from my mother and 23 chromosomes from my father united. At that, some would then assume, the genetic disorder was already in my parents and was passed down onto me: Nope, at least not in my case. Search Youtube for Jon Kolb, and you will see that he certainly does not have MD, and my mom does not have it either. No one in my family before me has had MD.

The MD spontaneously mutated in me at the moment of conception. And the reason I still have it, although I have prayed to God to heal me, is that He simply wants me to have it for some reason that will serve for the good. He has another plan for my life, and this is simply the cross I have to bear and the cup I have to drink. So, why should any of this be helpful? Because it is important to know the mind and will of God. If you have a chronic disease, something that the doctors cannot fix. Then pray to God and ask Him to heal you. To do that, you do not have to send money to anyone or go anywhere special and do anything in particular. Right here and now, you can ask God to heal you. And you can ask Him again and again. But do not give up living while waiting for healing. Continue to live. Keep moving forwards despite your illness, and you just may come to understand what 2. Cor.12: 9-10 truly means: "...My grace is sufficient for you, for my power is make perfect in weakness." Therefore I will boast all the more gladly about my weaknesses so that Christ's power may rest on me. That is why, for Christ's sake, I delight in weaknesses, in insults, in hardships, in persecutions, in difficulties. For when I am weak, then I am strong."

If that makes no sense to you at all, perhaps Romans 5:3-5 will help:

> "...we also glory in our sufferings, because we know that suffering produces perseverance, perseverance, character; and character, hope. And hope does not put us to shame, because God's love has been poured out into our hearts through the Holy Spirit, who has been given to us."

These verses in correlation with 1. Cor. 10: 13 assure us that whatever we are going through, illness, divorce, loss, whatever the source of pain maybe, if we trust in God, be obedient to His Holy Spirit, then we can just sit back and wade in the wonders of His majesty amid catastrophe. I have said it before, and I will say it again. I love facing problems because that is when I see God work in me and through me. When everything is going great without a trouble in the world, then motivation seems to fall. And when our behaviors lack motivation, they are very unlikely to become productive behaviors. It is a well known psychological fact that a significant amount of stress is beneficial. Studies comparing performance with stress have so distinctly determined that performance is the highest under moderate stress and the lowest under high and low stress that it has become common knowledge. The amount of stress that anyone has to deal with is solely subjective to that person. Still, if the stress is amounting to significant problems, then that needs to be dealt with. Begin by separating your problems from your facts, as discussed previously. Go to the doctors, pray for healing, ask others to pray for you. And when you have done all that, know that "No temptation has overtaken you except what is common to mankind. And God is faithful; he will not let you be tempted beyond what you can bear. But when you are tempted, he will also provide a way out so that you can endure it" (1. Cor.10:13, NIV).

I would like to think that I spend much of my time in life pondering the question, "how am I living?". In doing so, during this time of contemplation, it is as if I am not living in this life but rather find myself outside of it in self-reflection. At this moment, I am no longer in the game, I have called a time out, and I am talking with my coach about the current life situation. Because of this capacity, Paul claimed that we are no longer citizens of this world, but rather citizens of heaven. What I have come to realize is that we do not have to call a time out. Our citizenship is in heaven, the moment we accept Jesus as our Lord and Savior; and, we can have that right now, right here in this life. Most people see eternal salvation as the goal when, in reality, it is the starting line. We do not have to die to experience oneness with God. We can do that now, right now, through his Holy Spirit. We can live our lives right on earth as it is in heaven. And when we do this, our life on earth is absent of fear. Fear becomes what God intended it to be: a warning signal to keep us from doing stupid things.

In its purest form, as God intended it, fear is synonymous with respect. While the most frequent imperative in the Bible is 'fear not,' many scriptures such as Psalm 103:17, Psalm 112:1, Proverbs 9:10, and Matthew 10:28 state that we should fear God. Some would like to focus on the apparent contradiction, but it should be clear that the only kind of fear we should have for God is the purest, which is then merely respect. Indeed, God demands purity. Hence our fear for Him should be absolutely pure; and, this pureness is described through the term respect.

We know God is all-loving, but we also know what He did to the Egyptians, the Palestinians, Sodom and Gomorrah, the list goes one. Even clearer than God's love is God's power. Many would choose to question this, and indeed God has given a direct answer to those who would question his actions of destruction with respect to actions of blessings. One might ask, "God, are you sure you are doing this, right?" To which God responds, "Does not the potter have the right to make out of the same lump of clay some pottery for special purposes and some for common use? (Rom. 9:21). What is the difference between pottery for special purposes and some for common use? The difference is not in the beauty of the object or its worth. The difference is in the likely hood that it will be broken during its use. For the special pottery is placed in protection, and the other is used without further reflection or major concern. And when it breaks, we are more likely to mourn the loss of the common pottery's contents more than the pottery itself.

Essentially God is saying, "It is my creation, I can do what I want with it." Many people simply can not warm up to such a statement. It reminds me of our old backyard football games. The owner of the ball, or the owner of the backyard, had a significant influence on the outcome of any game because they could at any time call, "My ball/yard my rules." To this, all others had essentially three options: acceptance, challenge, or quit. I am extremely competitive, even aggressively competitive, so I always agreed to a do-over, welcoming the chance to assert my strength, with the attitude if you can do it once, you can do it again. Others would get so mad at the injustice that they would turn and walk away from the game. Occasionally, one would lash out at the injustice and fight.

I do not have a problem with God's statement, even if it does sound childish from a perspective. Childish or not, the statement is certainly true. And considering the three options of walking away from God, fighting Him, or simply being submissive to his rules, out of respect, I am going to go along with any and everything He wills. It boils down to this: Submission. When you experience this world, are you thankful for what you have, or are you spiteful for what you do not have? Do you blame God, yourself, or have you learned to live in forgiveness, love, and trust? God certainly has us in a difficult environment. How we respond to this environment through our behavior expresses who we are. We are either servants of God, who submit themselves to God, and say with all of our heart, body, mind, and soul, "I want for myself, only that what you want for me, my Lord." Or, we say this is my life, my heart, body, mind, and soul, and I will do with it what I want.

We are free to decide what we want for our lives. The profoundness of this statement is lost in its simplicity. Humans, and humans alone, are not totally mastered by their drives, instincts, and reflexes. We were created in the image of God for the purpose of a relationship with Him and His creation. We have the ability to suppress our animalistic instincts and decide for ourselves with conscious awareness of how we will react in any given situation. When we study the psychology of God, we gain a greater understanding of the significance of this process, and we begin to set our hearts and minds on things above instead of earthly things (Colossians 3:1-4).

> "Since, then, you have been raised with Christ, set your hearts on things above, where Christ is, seated at the right hand of God. Set your minds on things above, not on earthly things. For you died, and your life is now hidden with Christ in God. When Christ, who is your life, appears, then you also will appear with him in glory."

Author's Bio

Dr. Eric J. Kolb was born and raised on a farm in Nineveh, PA. His father was a professional football player for the Pittsburgh Steelers, and his mom was and still is a cowgirl. When He was two, he and his adopted sister were sleeping in their crib when a fire broke out. His dad was able to climb into a second-story window and save the two kids. Thus, Kolb grew up knowing that God had a special purpose for his life. In high school, Kolb started with a very promising future in sports, but injuries, most likely due to muscle dystrophy, led him down an academic path. Upon graduation with a bachelor's in Math from Ohio University, Kolb wanted to spend a summer in Germany as a street performer. Kolb became a professional performing artist, but once again, his illness changed his path. Thus, Kolb went back to school, obtained his master's in psychological counseling and later his Ph.D. in general psychology.

References

Ahmetoglu, G., Swami, V., & Chamorro-Premuzic, T. (2010). The relationship between dimensions of love, personality, and relationship length. *Arch. Sex. Behav.* 39:1181-1190. DOI 10.1007/s10508-009-9515-5.

Ai, A., Wink, P., & Shearer, M. (2011). Secular reverence predicts shorter hospital length of stay among middle-aged and older patients following open-heart surgery. *J. Behav. Med.* 34:532-541. DOI 10.1007/s10865-011-9334-8.

Aim A., Wink, P., Tice, T., Bolling,. & Shearer, M. (2009). Prayer and reverence in naturalistic, aesthetic, and socio-moral contexts predicted fewer complications following coronary artery bypass. *J. Behav. Med*, 32:570:581. DOI 10.1007/s10865-009-9228-1.

Bakker, A., Demerouti, E., & Sanz.Vergel, A. (2014). Burnout and work engagement: The JD-R approach. *Annu. Rev. Organ. Psychol. Organ. Behav.*, 1:389–411. DOI:10.1146/annurev-orgpsych-031413-091235.

Barnard, P., Duke, D., Byrne, R. & Davidson, I. (2007). Differentiation in cognitive and emotional meanings: An evolutionary analysis. *Cognition and emotion*, 21(6). DOI: 10.1080/02699930701437477.

Barrow, J. & Tipler, F. (2009). *The anthropic cosmological principle*. Oxford University Press: Oxford.

Bartussek, W. (2000). *Bewusst sein im Körper* [Consciousness in the body]. Mainz, Germany: Matthias-Grünewald-Verlag.

Beigl, H. (1952). The influence of body position on mental processes. *Journal of clinical Psychology*, 8(2), 193-199. DOI: 10.1002/1097-4679(195204)8:2<193::AID-JCLP2270080220>3.0.CO;2-.

Bekke-Hansen, S., Pedersen, C., Thygesen, K., Christensen, S., Waele, L. & Zachariae, R. (2012). *Complementary Therapies in Medicine*, 20, 306–315. DOI:10.1016/j.ctim.2012.03.003.

Berscheid, E. (1988). Some comments on love's anatomy: Or, whatever happened to old-fashioned lust? In R. Sternberg & M. Barnes (Eds.), The psychology of love (pp. 359–374). New Haven, CT: Yale University Press.

Blythe, Sally G. (2000). Early learning in the balance: priming the first ABC. *Support for Learning*, 15(4), pp. 154-158. Retrieved from PsychINFO.

Borneman, J., Gifford, A., Shively, M., Smith, T., Redwine, L., Kelly, A., Becker, S., Gershwin, M., Bone, P., & Belding, W. (2006). Effects of spiritual mantram repetition on HIV Outcomes: A Randomized controlled trial. *Journal of Behavioral Medicine, Vol. 29, No. 4, August 2006 (2006)* DOI: 10.1007/s10865-006-9063-6.

Broderick, Patricia C. & Blewitt, Pamela (2006). *The Life Span Human Development for Helping Professions Second Edition.* Pearson Education, Inc., Upper Saddle River, New Jersey.

Bucci, W. (1995). The power of the narrative: A multiple code account. In J.W. Pennebaker (Ed.). *Emotion, disclosure, & health* (pp. 93-122). Washington, DC: American Psychological Association. DOI:10.1037/10182-005.

Bucci, W. (2001). Pathways of emotional communication. *Psychoanalytic inquiry, 21*, 40–70. DOI: 10.1080/07351692109348923.

Bucci, W. (2002). The referential process, consciousness, and the sense of self. *Psychoanalytic inquiry.* 22(5), 166-794. DOI: 10.1080/07351692209349017.

Bucci, W. (2003). Varieties of dissociative experiences: A multiple code account and a discussion of Bromberg's case of "William." *Psychoanalytic psychology*, 20(3), 542-557. DOI: 10.1037/0736-9735.20.3.542.

Burger, K., & Samuel, R. (2017). The role of perceived stress and self-efficacy in young people's life satisfaction: A Longitudinal study. *Journal of Youth Adolescence*, 46, 78-90. DOI: 10.1007/s10964-016-0608-x.

Buss, D. (1999). *Evolutionary Psychology: The new science of the mind*. Needham Heights, MA: Allyn and Bacon.

Calvin (1996). *Institutes of the Christian Religion*. Volumes 1-4. Trans. Henry Beveridge. The Ages Digital Library, Theology.

Candada, A., Fltchett, G., Murphy, P., Stein, K., Portier, K., Crammer, C., & Peterman, A. (2013). Racial/ethnic differences in spiritual well-being among cancer survivors. *Jounal Behavioral Med.*, 36:441-453. DOI 10.1007/s10865-012-9439-8.

Cannon, W. (1927). *Bodily changes in pain, hunger, fear, and rage: An account of recent researches into the function of emotional excitement.* New York: D. Appleton and Company.

Carroll, J., & Russell, J. (1997). Facial expressions in Hollywood's portrayal of emotion. *Journal of personality and social psychology*, 72(1). http://dx.doi.org/10.1037/0022-3514.72.1.164

Chappell (1996). Why is faith a virtue? *Religious Studies*, 32(01), 27-36.

Chatters, L. M., Levin, J. S., & Taylor, R. J. (1992). Antecedents and dimensions of religious involvement among older Black adults. *Journal of Gerontology and Social Sciences*, 47B, S269–S278.

Clark, R. (2004). The classical origins of Pavlov's conditioning. *Integrative Physiological & Behavioral Science*, 39(4), 279-294.

Côté, J. E. (2006). Emerging Adulthood as an Institutionalized Moratorium: Risks and Benefits to Identity Formation. In J. J. Arnett & J. L. Tanner (Eds.), *Emerging adults in America: Coming of age in the 21st century* (p. 85–116). American Psychological Association. DOI: 10.1037/11381-004.

Damasio, A. (2000). *The feeling of what happens*. London: Heinemann.

Damasio, A. (2003). *Looking for Spinoza: Joy, sorrow, and the feeling brain*. London: William Heinemann.

Damasio, A. (2006). *Descartes' error: Emotion, reasoning, and the human brain*. London: Vintage Books.

Dawkins, R. (2006). *The blind watchmaker*. London: Penguin Books.

De Gelder, B. (2006). Towards the neurobiology of emotional body language. *Nature Reviews Neuroscience* 7(3), 242-249. Retrieved September 20, 2009 from Academic Search Premier.

De Maat, S., de Jonghe, F., & Schoevers, R., Dekker, J. (2009). The effectiveness of long-term psychoanalytic therapy: a systematic review of empirical studies. *Harv. Psychiatry,* 17(1):1-23. DOI: 10.1080/10673220902742476.

Diener, E., & Lucas, R. (1999). Personality and subjective well-being. In D. Kahneman, E. Diener & N. Schwarz (Eds.), Well-being: The foundations of the hedonic psychology (pp. 213–229). London: SAGE Publications.

Dimberg, U., Thunberg, M., & Elmehed, K. (2000). Unconscious facial reactions to emotional facial expressions. *Psychological science,* 11(1), 86-89. doi:10.1111/1467-9280.00221

Eccles (1989). *The evolution of the brain: Creation of the self.* New York: Routledge.

Edgar, I. I. (1935). Shakespeare's psychopathological knowledge: A study in criticism and interpretation. *The journal of abnormal and social psychology,* 30(1), 70-83. DOI:10.1037/h0059943.

Ekman, P. (2003). *Emotions revealed: Recognizing faces and feelings to improve communication and emotional life.* New York: Henry Holt.

Ekman, P. (2015). "Is Love an emotion?" E-mail from the Paul Ekman Group to Eric J. Kolb. Nov. 12, 2015.

Emanuele, E., Politi, P., Bianchi, M., Minoretti, P., Bertona, M., & Geroldi, D. (2006). Raised plasma nerve growth factor levels associated with early-stage romantic love. *Psychoneuroendocrinology,* 31, 288–294.

Feng, D., & Baker, L. (1994). Spouse similarity in attitudes, personality, and psychological well-being. *Behavior Genetics,* 24, 357– 364.

Fink, B. (2015). Love and/in Psychoanalysis: A commentary on Lacan's reading of Plato's symposium in seminar VIII: Transference. *Psychoanalytic Review,* 102(1).

Francis, S.A., Liverpool, J. A Review of Faith-Based HIV Prevention Programs. *J Relig Health* 48, 6–15 (2009). https://doi.org/10.1007/s10943-008-9171-4

Frankl, V. (1959). *Man's sSearch for Meaning: An introduction to logotherapy.* Boston: Beacon Press.

Führ, M. & Martin, R. (2002) *Coping Humor in early adolescence*. Humor 15-3, 283- 304. Retrieved on Feb. 7, 2008 from personal correspondence with Willibald Ruch.

Gardiner, H., Metcalf, R., & Beebe-Center, J. (1970). *Feeling and emotion: A history of theories*. Westport, Connecticut: Greenwood Press Publishers.

Gervais, W. (2012). Analytic thinking promotes religious disbelief. *Science*, 27 Apr. vol 336 Issue 6080. Pg. 493-496. DOI: 10.1126/science.1215647.

Giles, E. L., Sniehotta, F. F., McColl, E., & Adams, J. (2015). Acceptability of financial incentives and penalties for encouraging uptake of healthy behaviours: Focus groups. *BMC Public Health, 15* doi:http://dx.doi.org/10.1186/s12889-015-1409-y.

Gilligan, Carol (1982). *In a Different Voice*. Harvard University Press. Cambridge, Massachusetts, and London, Egland.

Gordon, R. M. (2006). What is love? Toward a unified model of love relations. *Psychoanalytic Psychology*, 28, 25–34.

Gosselin, P., Kirouas, G., & Dore, F. (1995). Components and recognition of facial expression in the communication of emotion by actors. *Journal of personality and social psychology, 68*(1). DOI: 10.1037/0022-3514.68.1.83.

Harris, V., & Katkin, E. (1975). Primary and secondary emotional behavior: An analysis of the role of autonomic feedback on affect, arousal, and attribution. *Psychological bulletin, 82*(6), 904-916. DOI: 10.1037/0033-2909.82.6.904.

Hatfield, G. (2007). Did Descartes have a Jamesian theory of the emotions? *Philosophical psychology, 20*(4), 413-440. doi: 10.1080/09515080701422041.

Haugan, G., Utvær, B., & Moksnes, U. (2013). The Herth Hope Index – A psychometric study among cognitively intact nursing home patients. Jorunal of Nursing measurement, 21(3), 378-400. http://dx.doi.org/10.1891/1061-3749.21.3.378.

Holt. Lunstad, J., Steffen, P., Sandberg, J., & Jensen, B. (2011). Understanding the connection between spiritual well-being and physical health: an examination of ambulatory blood pressure, inflammation, blood lipids and fasting glucose. *J Behav Med,* 34:477–488 DOI 10.1007/s10865-011-9343-7.

Holslander, L., Duggleby, W. Williams, A., Write, K. (2005). The experience of hopw for informal caregivers of Palliative Patients. *Journal of Palliative Care*, 21(4), 285-291. DOI: 10.1177/082585970502100408.

Izard, C. E. (1993). Four systems for emotional activation: Cognitive and noncognitive processes. *Psychological review*, 100(1), 68-90.

James, W. (1890). *The principles of psychology, Vol. 1-2*. New York: Dover Publications.

Johnstone, K. (1981). Status. In *Impro: Improvisation and the theatre*. England: Clay. Ltd.

Kepner, J. (2005). *Körper prozesse: Ein gestalttherapeutischer Ansatz*. (translated from Britte Stein: Body Process: A gestalt approach to working with the body in psychotherapy. New York: Verlag Garner Press, 1989). Bergisch Gladbach, ‚Germany: Verlag Andreas Kohlage.

King, L. A., Burton, C. M., Hicks, J. A., & Drigotas, S. M. (2007). Ghosts, UFOs, and magic:

Positive affect and the experiential system. *Journal of Personality and Social Psychology*, 92(5), 905-919. DOI: 10.1037/0022-3514.92.5.905.

Klaver, J., Lee, Z., & Hart, S. (2007). Psychopathy and nonverbal indicatiors of deception in offenders. *Law Hum Behav*, 31:337-351. DOI: 10.1007/s10979-006-9063-7.

Klaver, J., Lee, Z., Spindel, A., & Hart, S. (2009). Psychopathy and deception detection using indirect measures. *Legal and Criminological Psychology*, 14, 171-182. DOI: 10.1348/135532508X289964.

Kochanska, G., Aksan, N., & Joy, M. (2007). Children's fearfulness as a moderator of parenting in early socialization: Two longitudinal studies. *Developmental Psychology*, 43(1), 222–237. DOI: 10.1037/0012-1649.43.1.222

Kolb, E. (2010). Status: The basic grammar of non verbal communication. In *Researchgate.net*. http://www.researchgate.net/publication/320842649_Status_The_Basic_Grammar_of_Nonverbal_Communication

Kolb, E. (2013). The definition of humor: A New Perspective. https://www.researchgate.net/publication/256503346_The_definition_of_humor_A_New_Perspective

Kolb, E. (2017). Directed expression: Quantifying emotional expression with concepts derived from the performing arts. https://www.researchgate.net/publication/314114921_Directed_expression_Quantifying_emotional_expression_with_concepts_derived_from_the_performing_arts

Krauss, L. (2012). *A universe from nothing: Why there is something rather than nothing.* London: Simon & Schuster.

Kuilema, J. (2014). Faith as virtue in social work practice: A reformed perspective. *Social Work & Christianity*, 41(2-3), 155-174. ISSN: 0737-5778.

Kuiper, N. & Martin, R. (1993). Coping humor, stress, and Cognitive Appraisals. *Canadian Journal of Behavior Science*, 25(1), 81-96.

Kuiper, N. & Sorrel, N. (2004). Thoughts of feeling better? Sense of humor and Physical health. *Humor*, 17(1/2), 37-66.

Kuiper, N., Grimshaw, M. Leite, C. & Gillian, K. (2004). Humor is not always the best medicine: Speific components of sense of humor and psychological well-being. *Humor*, 17(1/2), 135-168.

Lazarus, R. (1975). A cognitively oriented psychologists looks as biofeedback. *American Psychologist*, 30(5), 553–561. https://doi.org/10.1037/h0076649.

Lazarus, R. (1982). Thoughts on the relations between emotion and cognition. *American psychologist*, 37(9), 1019-1024. doi:10.1037/0003-066X.37.9.1019.

Lazarus, R. (1991). Cognition and motivation in emotion. *American psychologist*, 46(4), 352-367. doi:10.1037/0003-066X.46.4.352.

Martikainen, L. (2009). The many faces of life satisfaction among Finnish Young Adults. *Journal of Happiness Studies*, 10:721-737. DOI 10.1007/s10902-008-9117-2

Martin, R. (2007). *The psychology of humor an integrative approach.* Elsevier Academic Press, London, UK.

Milgram, S. (1963). Behavioral study of obedience. Journal of Abnormal and social Psychology, 67(4), 371-378. DOI: 10.1037/h0040525.

Moksnes, U.K., Espnes, G.A. Self-esteem and life satisfaction in adolescents—gender and age as potential moderators. *Qual Life Res* **22**, 2921–2928 (2013). https://doi.org/10.1007/s11136-013-0427-4.

Navarro, J., & Karlins, M. (2008). *What every body is saying.* New York: Harper Collins Books.

Neenan, M. & Dryden W. (2004). *Cognitive Therapy - 100 key points and techniques.* New York: Brunner- Routledge.

Newberg, A. & Waldman, M. (2009). *How God Changes your Brain.* New York: Ballantine Books Trade Paperbacks.

Newlin, K., Dyess, S., Allard, E., Chase, S., & Mulkus, G. (2011). A methodological review of faith-based health promotion literature: Advancing the science to expand delivery of diabetes education to black Americans. *Journal of Religious Health*, 51: 1075-1097. DOI: 10.2003/s10943-011-9481-9.

Nezlek, J. & Derks, P. (2001). Use of humor as a coping mechanism, psychological adjustment, and social interaction. *Humor* (14)4, 395-413. Retrieved November 18, 2007 from EbscoHost database.

Nezu, A., Nezu, C., & Blissett, S. (1988). Sense of humor as a moderator of the relation between stressful events and psychological distress: A prospective analysis. *Journal of Personality and Social Psychology*, 54(3), 520-525.

Norcross, J. (2002). *Psychotherapy relationships that work.* New York: Oxford University Press.

Nussbaum (2003). *Brain health and wellness.* ISBN: 1932205640, 9781932205640

O'Connor, T. G. (2006). Toward Integrating Behavior Genetics and Family Process. Family *Systems, & Health,* 24(4), 416-424. DOI: 10.1037/1091-7527.24.4.416.

Öhman, A., Lundqvist, D., & Esteves, F. (2001). The face in the crowd revisited: A threat advantage with schematic stimuli. *Journal of Personality and Social Psychology,* 80(3), 381–396. https://doi.org/10.1037/0022-3514.80.3.381

Peacocke, A. (1993). Theology for a scientific age: Being and becoming – natural, divine, and human, in *Theology and the sciences*. Minneapolis: Fortress Press.

Pedersen, C., Christensen, S., Jensen, A., & Zachariae (2013). In god and CAM we trust. Religious Faith and use of complementary and alternative medicine (CAM) in a nationwide cohort of women treated for early breast cancer. Journal of Religious Health, 52:991-1013. DOI 10.1007/s10943-012-9569-x.

Pennycook, G., Cheyne, J., Seli, P., Koehler, D., & Fugelsang, J. (2012). Analytic cognitive style predicts religious and paranormal belief. *Cognition*, 123, 335-346.

Plomain R., Reiss, D. Hetherington, E. & Howe, G. (1994). Nature and Nurture: Genetic Contributions to Measures of the Family Environment. *Developmental Psychology*, 30(1), 32-43.

Pope, D. & Whiteley, H. (2003). Developmental dyslexia, cerebellar/vestibular brain function and possible links to exercise-based interventions: A review. *European Journal of Special Needs Education*, 18,(1), 109-123. doi: 10.1080/0885625032000042348.

Rabbit, P., Lunn., M., Ibrahim, S., Cobain, M., & McInnes, L. (2007). Unhappiness, health, and cognitive ability in old age. *Psychological Medicine*, 38, 229-236. DOI: 10.1017/S0033291707002139.

Ratey (2008). *Spark: The revolutionary new science of exercise & the brain*. New York: Luttle Brown.

Redfern, R. (2012). *The Childhood experience of attention deficit hyperactivity disorder*. A Dissertation Pacifica Graduate Institute, Doctor of Philosophy in clinical psychology.

Reiss, S. (2000). *Who am I? The 16 basic desires that motivate our action and define our personalities*. New York: Berkley Publishing Group.

Ritchie, G. (2004). Reinterpretation and viewpoints. *Humor*, 19(3), 251-270.

Robert Sapolsky (2004). *Why Zebras Don't get ulcers*. St. Matin Press : New York.

Rogers, C. (1951). *Client-centered therapy: Its current practice, implications, and theory*. Boston: Houghton Mifflin Company.

Rogers, C. (2007). The necessary and sufficient conditions of therapeutic personality change. *Psychotherapy: Theory, Research, Practice, Training, 44*(3), 240–248 DOI: 10.1037/0033-3204.44.3.240

Rojas, M. (2006). Life satisfaction and satisfaction in domains of life: Is it a simple relationship? *Journal of Happiness Studies, 7,* 467-497. DOI: 10.1007/s10902-006-9009-2.

Ruch, W. (Ed.) (1998). *The sense of humor: Explorations of a personality characteristic.* Berlin: Mouton de Gruyter.

Schramm, R. (2006). *Motivation and reinforcement: turning the tables on autism.*

Shenhav, A.; Rand, D., & Greene, J. (2012). Divine intuition: Cognitive style influences belief in God. *Journal of Experimental Psychology: General, 141*(3), 423-428. DOI: 10.1037/a0025391.

Sherman, A., Simonton, S., Latif, U., Spohn, R., & Tricot, G. (2005). Religious Struggle and Religious Comfort in Response to Illness: Health Outcomes among Stem Cell Transplant Patients. *Journal of Behavioral Medicine, Vol. 28, No. 4.* DOI: 10.1007/s10865-005-9006-7

Sieratzki, J. & Woll, B. (1996). Why do mothers cradle babies on their left?. *The Lancet, 347*(9017), 1746-1748. https://doi.org/10.1016/S0140-6736(96)90813-2.

Skinner, B. (1938). *The behavior of organisms: An experimental analysis.* New York: Appleton-Century-Crofts, Inc.

Steiner, R. (1918). *Ancient Myths: Their Meaning and Connection with Evolution,* Steiner Book Centre: Toronto, Canada.

Swami, V., Stieger, S., Haubner, T., Voracek, M., & Furnham, A. (2009). Evaluating the physical attractiveness of oneself and one's romantic partner: Individual and relationship correlates of the love- is-blind bias. *Journal of Individual Differences, 30,* 35–43.

The Colour Works. (2011). Hippocrates – Greek Physician. http://www.thecolourworks.com/hippocrates-galen-the-four-humours/

Tjeltveit, A. C. (2006). Psychology's love-hate relationship with love: Critiques, affirmations, and Christian responses. *Journal of Psychology and Theology, 34,* 8–22.

Tsai, J. &Rosenheck, R. (2011). Religiosity among adults who are chronically homeless: Association with clinical and psychosocial outcomes. *Psychiatric Services*, 62(10), 1222-1224.

Veenhoven, R: (1996). Developments in satisfaction research. *Social Indicators Research*, 37,1–45.

Veenhoven, R. (1991). Is happiness relative? *Social Indicators Research*, 24, 1–34.

Warner-Rogers, J., Taylor, A., Taylor, E. & Sandberg, S. (2000). Inattentive Behavior in Childhood: Epidemiology and implications for development. *Journal of Learning Disabilities*, 33(4), pp. 520-536.

Westmacott, R. (2011). Reasons for terminating psychotherapy: Client and therapist perspectives. Dissertation Doctor of Philosophy in clinical Psychology.

White , K. (2001). Revolution for the human spirit. *Organization Developmental Journal*, 19(2), 47-58.

Wild, B., Rodden, F., Grodd, W., & Ruch, W. (2003). Neural correlates of laughter and humor. *Brain*, 126, 1-18.

Zeidner, M. & Kaluda, I. (2008). Romantic love: What's emotional intelligence (EI) got to do with it? Personality and Individual Differences, 44(8), 1684-1695. DOI: 10.1016/j.paid.2008.01.018.

Zuckerman, M. (1999). *Vulnerability to Psychopathology: A Bilsocial Model*. American Psychological Association. Washington D.C.

Zweyer, Karen, Barbara Velker, and Willibald Ruch. HUMOR: International Journal of Humor Research. 17.1- 2 (2004): 67-84.

CPSIA information can be obtained
at www.ICGtesting.com
Printed in the USA
BVHW091402040221
599123BV00004B/6